T0355390

LEARNING IN A
TIME OF
ABUNDANCE

LEARNING IN A TIME OF ABUNDANCE

The Community Is the Curriculum

DAVE CORMIER

JOHNS HOPKINS UNIVERSITY PRESS
Baltimore

© 2024 Johns Hopkins University Press
All rights reserved. Published 2024
Printed in the United States of America on acid-free paper
2 4 6 8 9 7 5 3 1

Johns Hopkins University Press
2715 North Charles Street
Baltimore, Maryland 21218
www.press.jhu.edu

Library of Congress Cataloging-in-Publication Data is available.

A catalog record for this book is available from the British Library.

ISBN 978-1-4214-4779-7 (hardcover)
ISBN 978-1-4214-4780-3 (ebook)

*Special discounts are available for bulk purchases of this book. For more information,
please contact Special Sales at specialsales@jh.edu.*

For my mother, who still teaches me how to face uncertainty

CONTENTS

ACKNOWLEDGMENTS

First, I'd like to thank my family for supporting me through all the whinging and revising and self-doubt that accompanied the writing of this book. To Bonnie, who is my life partner and also my thinking partner: thanks for giving me the space to write and for the thousand conversations we've had that have helped the ideas in this book get better. And to Wren and Josephine, our kids: thank you for keeping me grounded and intellectually honest, and for letting me sound out many of the ideas in this book.

I am grateful to Lawrie Phipps and John Schinker, who read every word of this book (more than once) as I was trying to write it, and who pushed me to finish it. To Autumm Caines, my sister Cindy, my cousin Michele Doiron, Daniel Lynds, Lee Skallerup Bessette, Heather Carroll, Ashlyne O'Neil, and the many others whose offers to help and to read and whose prompting have been so important to the development of the book.

Thanks to my peeps at the University of Windsor for being supportive of this project. Nick Baker and the rest of the Office of Open Learning team have been super patient with me as I've blabbed about this project over the course of four years. To Greg and the fine folks at Johns Hopkins University Press for believing in this project, and the amazing editors at Inksplash who very, very patiently helped me clarify the story I was trying to tell.

This book wouldn't exist without the excellent community of educators in my community. There are so many people whom I've been fortunate to work with and learn from over the years. How do you list a community that has extended over almost twenty years, through MOOCs, EdTechTalk, and dozens of events and great discussions? Thanks to Olga Ioannou, Maha Bali, George Siemens, Laura Gogia, Jim Luke, Martin Weller, Sarah Rose Cavanagh, Rebecca Petersen, Giulia Forsythe, Beyhan Farhadi, Lenandlar Singh, Aras Bozkurt, Jeff Lebow, Darcy Norman, Alan Levine, Kristen Lwin, Jim Groom, Brian Lamb, Kate Bowles, Jennifer Maddrell, Mita Williams, Terry Greene, and Ken Montgomery (who will read this all again, with citations, in my thesis), and so many hundreds of others. My community has always been my curriculum, and I have learned so much from all of you.

Finally, to my father, who never got to see this book finished. You did good. Rest.

LEARNING IN A TIME OF ABUNDANCE

Introduction

On a cold December morning in 1998, I found myself on the wrong side of a locked door on my way to teach my first-ever class. The class was scheduled to start in twenty minutes, and not a single teacher or child was anywhere in sight. I'd had about a week of teacher training from a course I took before leaving Canada, and I was just trying to make enough money to travel. As a newly arrived foreigner in Busan, South Korea, I was not really prepared to be in charge of a room full of five-year-olds.

I soon found out that I was scheduled to teach the letter *h*. I have spoken English all my life, but that first morning, I couldn't remember an *h* word that I had any chance of describing to a room full of children who didn't speak English. Words flickered through my mind: *helicopter, heliotrope, homogeneous*. But not, from what I can recall, a word like *hat*. One of the kids pulled out their textbook and pointed (I still think it was out of pity), and I was saved. There it was in black and white at the front of the chapter: the familiar lines of a house that I could draw on the whiteboard.

I caught the teaching bug that day. I loved the challenge of it: confronting the weirdness of the English language while trying to connect with the small humans in front of me. Eventually, I moved on from teaching little children to a junior college. I also shifted from teaching the textbook that was lying in front of me to selecting resources that seemed to fit what I was trying to do. I started asking all the questions that a new teacher asks, often quietly, to themselves, where no one can hear them. What English was I supposed to teach? What sense did it make to grade their attempts at speaking one version of English? I was invested in the art of education.

I was also disorganized, and over the following years, I found myself mournfully confronting the paper detritus of hundreds of students all over my desk. So, despite being a computer science dropout, I turned to a computer for help. I began "teaching online" in the very early 2000s, mostly out of desperation: my students and I still met face-to-face in a classroom, but I had them post their work online so that I wouldn't lose their assignments. I didn't have to shuffle through the thousands of pieces of paper strewn around my office and crumpled up in the bottom of my briefcase.

Given that we were already working on the web, I asked my students to find things to read online too. They came back from their web searches with surprises. They found idioms I couldn't explain—*the skin of your teeth*, for one—and asked about them. They stumped me. In this case, they weren't wrong: teeth don't have skin. I could see the suspicious look in their eyes when they realized that I didn't know the answer. The phrase was English.

I was the English teacher. How could I not know what something meant in English?

My teaching world changed when I moved online. I was far more organized in collecting students' work, but my teaching was more uncertain. The simple confidence that I'd found using that first textbook had gone away. I didn't always know what was going to happen in my classrooms. I stopped using a textbook and increasingly relied on the web. I had lots of things I *could* teach but was often at a loss about where to start. And my students had information at their fingertips—often more information than I had.

If you are not teaching with a textbook, how do you know what you're supposed to teach? In a subject as varied and unreliable as the English language, what do you encourage students to focus on? How do you decide who or what is right? Once you are no longer constrained by which printed book can be accessed in a classroom, the job of teaching changes. There is research a teacher can do, certainly; but I didn't really know anything about that back then.

A teacher grappling with uncertainty forces students to grapple with it, too. Sure, there were some students who enjoyed the freedom to choose the pieces they were going to read or work on; but many did not. Contrary to my expectation, not all my students liked to make random choices the same way I did (embarrassing to admit now, but I totally didn't understand that at the time). And choice is what the internet is going to give you, whether you want it or not.

Teaching and learning in my classroom certainly felt different the more I used the internet—less certain but more exploratory. But what do we do with that feeling? How do we think about what it means to learn in ways that are different than the ones we were taught before the web existed? I've been chasing how to describe that feeling and talk about its implications ever since.

The question is not whether we should use the internet or if teaching with books is better. The internet exists. This cultural shift has happened. We are not living in a world where we turn to physical books to try to find answers to most of our questions. I do still look to them for inspiration. And I still read my carpentry books for reference because I don't find that my computer likes the woodshop dust very much. But most of the time, I search the web.

Here's the question: Is having the internet a small change when it comes to how we learn things, or is it a transformational change? Is the change comparable to the popularization of the interlibrary loan system, or is it as dramatic as the invention of the printing press? If the change really is transformational, then is it a big enough change for us to have to come up with new ways of thinking about what it means to learn and to have learned? What does it even mean to have learned? I have a sense of what it meant to me in my childhood, but could I write it out in a way that would encompass all that it means?

What the internet does do is ramp up the choices that we have. The uncertainty I first saw in my classrooms in the early 2000s is increasingly a part of everyone's daily lives. In so many different ways, we are moving away from that "one way" to do things, toward having a multitude of options, whether we are trying to make a pasta sauce or figure out who to vote for. When we look around ourselves right now, it's hard to know what to believe. It used to be that if it came from a published book or from someone who was famous enough to be on TV, then we had a good chance of it being true or maybe at least useful. Now for every question we have, there are hundreds, maybe thousands, of different answers.

Well. Not every question. There are certainly things that have clear answers. We have names for animals. We have all decided to drive on the left (or right, depending on where you are) side of the street. There are lots of things that are either objectively true or that we've all decided we'll do the same way. That's fine. There are facts. We all certainly don't agree on what might constitute a fact and what things can be facts. But let's at least agree that they exist. I don't think the idea that we disagree on what constitutes a fact or that facts exist changed with the arrival of more information.

What about those questions that go beyond the realm of facts—the challenges that we have to face and need to make decisions about? How do we connect to our community? What will we do when we run out of cobalt? What should we choose to eat? How do we feel about burning carbon for fuel? What do children need to know to become successful adults?

It is hard, above all, to know how to decide.

These are all questions that were once decided by family custom, by what we believed, and by where we lived. You voted like your family voted. You ate the food that grew in your region when it could be eaten or you made a special effort to bring food in. It used to be that we had a pretty narrow field for decision making. A narrow set of points upon which to decide. A scarcity of information. A scarcity of inputs.

But now we are part of everything that happens. We are witnesses for every event in every part of the world. I can see where rainforests have been cut down. I can hear the concerns of people who think I should eat organically . . . or locally. And we, ourselves, are a part of that abundance of information. Every time we repost something on Facebook or like something on Instagram, we amplify a given message, we lend it our credibility, and we add to the noise. To some extent, the louder voice has always won, I suppose; but now, from an information standpoint, there's loud everywhere.

It is overwhelming.

There also seems to be some expectation, at least culturally, that all of us should have an opinion on every one of these issues. Not only "Oh yes, I have heard about this issue, and it does sound important" either. We are often expected to weigh in on each issue with an informed position, leading to an attempt to have a position on thousands of issues or simply tuning out because you just can't bear to have a position on yet another issue. And there are so many issues.

I don't think this response is accidental. I think there's a connection between the way we've been taught to learn and the way we handle the world around us—the way we talk to each other, the way we make important decisions in our lives, and the way we confront all of the uncertainties in our everyday lives.

Although our ways of thinking about how we learn may not have adapted to the abundance around us, the way people try to influence us certainly has. Huge shifts in learning have happened before; and when they happened, new opportunities and problems presented themselves. Some people saw these opportunities and took advantage of the new landscape—and of other people along with it. Companies, political parties, and others have realized that they can use this new way of learning and new abundance to latch on to our uncertainty for their own benefit.

I don't think we're ready.

There's a bookshelf next to the couch where my partner and I do all of our writing. It is a carefully curated (not by me) collection that includes books we read and loved as kids, books we cite now, and reference books our children pull off the shelves on a daily basis. While I was sitting there in the quiet of cat fur, trying to start this story, my hand pulled out Stuart Ewen's excellent book *PR! A Social History of Spin*. It's a history of how marketing developed, mostly starting in the early 1900s when we had new communication tools, like radio, that allowed for new kinds of connections and messaging.

In the first few pages of the well-worn paperback, I returned to Ewen's first conversation with the granddaddy of modern marketing, Edward Bernays. Bernays is the guy who convinced the suffragette marchers in New York City to hold up their cigarettes as "torches of freedom" and started a dozen other marketing techniques that we all now take for granted. He was a magician of tying a feeling to a brand. In reflecting on his conversation with Bernays, Ewen says, "Ideally, the job of public relations is not simply one of disseminating favorable images and impressions for a client. For Bernays and, as I would learn, for many others in the field, the goal was far more ambitious. Public relations was about fashioning and projecting credible renditions of reality itself."

Bernays was looking to make an updated, credible rendition of reality for his clients. Think of the De Beers ad that led to the belief that a wedding ring should cost two months' salary. All through my childhood, I heard references to the financial straits of men trying to buy an engagement ring for their fiancée. It's a TV trope. Why was it two months' salary? Why was it a standard for decades?

I suppose it's possible that the company cared about marriages and thought they'd be better with diamonds. But it was very lucrative for De Beers to make people believe that. The marketing company made people believe it was "true" or, more specifically, that it was "what was done"—a reality. I mean, if you didn't buy a real diamond, you clearly didn't care enough about your future wife.

And why did we believe it? Before 1930 there was no particular connection between a diamond ring and a wedding. There certainly wasn't a sense of how much of one's salary should be spent on a ring. There are no religious texts that stipulate that a person needs a piece of hardened carbon attached to a ring of gold to give to someone before marrying them. It's not even a symbol of marriage; it's a symbol of almost-marriage. And yet, at least in the United States and Canada, it became the norm.

Marketing is so ingrained in our culture—so normal—that it's easy to overlook. Think of the ways in which marketing tries to associate us with brands. Most of us have accepted the idea that we should have the names of car companies on our cars. We pay them piles of money and then we drive our cars around and advertise for them. We do this, partially, because those brand associations mean something to people. People with a PC laptop generally say "laptop," whereas people with Apple products say "MacBook Pro." Our product choices say something about us. If you see a person with a Ford F-150 or a Toyota Prius, there are assumptions you might make about them. I'm not saying that all people who own those cars are the same type of person, or that your assumptions will be right. Those things are all just a part of our public identities. But there are thoughts and feelings associated with them. Those thoughts are carefully crafted by car companies' marketing groups to sell cars.

The marketing companies have made those things true. They have consciously associated women smoking with emancipation. They have consciously created campaigns to encourage people to believe that diamond rings should cost a kazillion dollars and be given as almost-married gifts. They have consciously shaped the kind of person who would drive a given vehicle. They are makers of truth.

Those marketers took advantage of a new technology (radio) to find a new way to teach us things. They told us what the right things were. They weren't necessarily things that we asked to learn. They weren't, in some cases, even things we knew we were learning, but we learned them. And all that using radio.

And I'm going to argue that we've been taught to respond to this kind of "truth." Our systems of learning are designed around rewarding people for getting the answer "right." More problematically, they are designed around someone else telling people whether they got the right answer. Think of almost any classroom you've ever been in. Someone else asked the questions. Someone else told you that you approached the question the right way. Someone else told you that you got it right. You were being taught a curriculum that was decided upon elsewhere, for *reasons*.

It's not just the things already in the world that are part of this new infrastructure. We are part of that abundance of information that surrounds us. Accessing and creating information has become an afterthought—it's something we do on purpose, by mistake, or sometimes by doing nothing at all. A small flutter across my keyboard gets me instructions for making a sourdough starter. I can pull up an app that will tell me where to get a decent glass of beer or better coffee in most cities I've ever visited.

Every time I launch an app or search Google Maps, the GPS is activated, telling someone somewhere about what I'm doing. It might tell them what I'm searching for, what things I'm clicking, or where I am. The information is put into a box somewhere. Maybe no one looks at it. Maybe someone does look at it and decides what kind of beer people like. Those pioneers of radio marketing were only shouting into the void. Imagine what they could have done with this much direct feedback.

Is this a problem?

Well, that depends. If you are trying to make delicious bread, it is decidedly not a problem. You can find a recipe and make some bread, and someone else knows about it. You're probably going to post a picture of your bread anyway, so who cares if a company somewhere knows about it. If, on the other hand, you are worried that young white males are being targeted by racist groups and being encouraged into violent acts, then it is a very great problem indeed. Those bits of information that we are giving out make that targeting much more effective.

Both of these outcomes come from the way the internet works. It is where we are. Things have changed around us whether we recognize the ways those changes are affecting our culture or not.

Some of the changes are big and some are subtle. At the very least, my ability to reach into my pocket and get the answer to many yes/no questions changes the value of being able to remember that information. I can spell now, even if it's with the help of a spellchecker. The fact that a doctor can pull up the most recent research on a rare disease from the side of a hospital bed changes what it means to be a doctor and, probably, should change the way doctors are taught. It also means that a doctor can glance over a piece of research without thinking very much about it and make some bad decisions with that information.

From a learning perspective, we've run up against a real problem. That problem, simply stated, is that our education system was designed to teach people to remember things in a world where information was hard to come by. That education system, to be fair, is at least partially responsible for you being able to read this book. The mandatory "educating of people" began for a pile of different reasons, but whatever your beliefs, students go to school to prepare for something. Society wanted the learners to know certain things that were going to help someone, be it the learners or someone else in that society.

One of the most important things we learned as students in school was how to learn. If we learned by finding an authority (our teacher, a book) and trusting that authority, then that's going to impact how we approach learning now. We're going to find someone or something that can tell us what to believe, remember that thing, and be rewarded for believing it. But what if there are 1,000 authorities and a million websites? How do we find the trusted authority when the information is everywhere? We still need to choose what to do. How do we face this uncertainty?

One way we can go about it is that we can look for experts and ask them for advice. We can ask the "technology people" what to do about living in the world we find ourselves in. Down that road, we have a future dominated by entrepreneurs in Silicon Valley—people who are committed to tracking you and using your data in innovative ways to make money. We have been walking down this path. It is jammed full of consultants who are telling us that the next innovation is the one we have to care about. Artificial intelligence. Personalized learning. I have heard their keynotes. They are selling something, and it is not a prosocial society or a form of learning that I would have hoped for. They are talking about what the technology can do, but they are not talking about what the technology and its impacts mean. They do not get rewarded for helping; they get rewarded for making money.

A second path is the straight path—the one that has us holding tight to the cart, blinders on. We just go along with the things we acquire. We step away from Facebook and don't get a Wi-Fi connection on the dishwasher. (I'm frankly still not sure why I would want Wi-Fi on my dishwasher.) When pressed to change, we slowly integrate into our lives the new technologies that allow us to do the exact same thing we were doing before . . . but faster. We collaborate on Google Docs. We use ChatGPT to write our application letter for a new job. We ask Google the answer to one of our yes/no questions. This path is by far the easiest because it has the weight of inertia to it.

Neither of these paths addresses the issue at hand: How has all of this information and connection changed what it means to be good friends, parents, teachers, bosses, and citizens? Many of us are struggling to come to terms with our own place inside the new reality. Do I take my phone to the bathroom with me? How should I be supervising my teen's internet use? Should I get an Amazon Echo in my house? Do I spend too many hours playing Candy Crush? Do I care how much data Gmail takes from me in exchange for functional email? Should I chime in on that nasty thread I just saw on Facebook? Should I really be worried about fluoride in my drinking water hurting my kids or aluminum cooking pots causing Alzheimer's? Is that video of my favorite political candidate a deepfake, or did they really say that awful thing?

Some of these questions have actual answers, even if they are difficult to discover and require us to sift through endless competing narratives. Many of them are questions that require us to ask ourselves what kind of world we want to live in. What we value.

Alone and together, we have lost control of parts of our cultural narrative. Things have changed enough that we need to think differently about what it means to learn and to have learned, and about how we make decisions in the world we live in. I'm not talking about how super scientists or chess players learn; I'm talking about the everyday kind of learning we need to do to get by.

We need to change the way we think about the reality we are in . . . and we need as many people as possible to pull together in that effort. Already, many of our inherited, commonsense instincts don't take into account this new reality. We are confronted with more decisions, more information, and more people trying to sell us things. Where can we turn for a trusted voice? Who is going to tell us that we got the right answer?

Let's think for a minute about that doctor looking at their phone as they sit by your bedside. I'm not suggesting that medical schools need to teach that doctor how to do a search for diseases or that we give them a list of trusted websites they need to use for their work, though those are probably good ideas. I am also not suggesting that the doctor needs a "Doctors.Social" account to connect to other doctors and crowdsource a differential diagnosis on the patient. I'm saying that for the doctor to do the best job possible, we, the patients, all need to think about how that doctor learns differently.

Think about it: You're sitting on a hospital bed and a young doctor walks in, asks you a few questions, and then does a quick search on their phone. What are you thinking? *Don't they know what's wrong with me? Didn't they learn to be a doctor when they were in medical school? Can someone please find me a doctor who knows what they're doing? Can't they check Instagram on their own time?*

Because that doctor has been to medical school, we feel like they should have learned all they needed to learn to attend to our illness. That's what a doctor is after all: someone who got through doctor school. Yes, they have a medical license and all; but for most of us, a doctor = a person who made it through medical school. All of the testing that was done in their medical school education has proven that they've learned what they need to know. If they had done all their studying, then they should be able to tell us what's wrong with us. I mean, they passed, didn't they?

Funny thing is, if we dig a little deeper, that belief doesn't live by itself. In our first of many moments of cognitive dissonance in this book, we know we hold opposing beliefs. Would you like to be treated with the medications that your sixty-year-old doctor learned about in medical school? No, you expect them to be up to date with the latest treatments, and that knowledge requires doctors to learn all the time. But the idea that a doctor is just supposed to *know* is deeply ingrained. That knowing is synonymous with remembering. If you need to look it up, you don't remember it; and if you don't remember it, you don't know it.

Canadian medical educators I've talked to will tell you that you don't even really "learn" to be a doctor until you do your practical, in-hospital work in your third year. And not until you do your residency after you become an MD do you really understand how to be a doctor. Most doctors believe that you learn about being a doctor on the job, working with patients, surrounded by other people more experienced than you who are doing a little cross-reference on the medication you just prescribed. For them, the community of doctors and patients is the curriculum of becoming a doctor.

Our disdain for the doctor checking their phone doesn't really match up with our understanding of the world. Yes, we want doctors to know things. Yes, we want them to grow in their knowledge. We just don't want them growing in their knowledge in front of us, where we can see it.

There's also the question of how a doctor deals with the modern patient who spent twenty hours on Google before they walked through their office door. Maybe they used the new AI chatbot, asked it about their symptoms, and just came into the hospital for a prescription for the disease they are now sure they have. That patient could very well know more about the treatments for their ailment than the doctor does. Or, far more likely, there's the patient who feels like they know more than their doctor does and has read some random things on the internet. Patients are increasingly coming into offices and emergency rooms demanding certain treatments and refusing others. What is the voice they are trusting? Is it their friends? Random algorithms? Is it coming through advertisements?

The tricky thing about those advertisements is that they no longer sound like the soap ads from the 1940s. They aren't merely a thirty-second spot on TV or a billboard on the highway. The advertisement is increasingly integrated. Paid time during the evening newscast made to look like a news story. A

Facebook post shared by your daughter. An ad targeted at you because you talked about having a sore shoulder near your Alexa. Being impacted by marketing is still learning, it's just learning for someone else's benefit.

The abundance of information changes learning for the doctor, for the patient, for the medical school, and for us on the sidelines. The patient has "learned" about their ailment. The doctor has "learned" about it and could learn more about it from their search. Does the new abundance of information mean we should trust doctors less than we did before, or does it simply expose us to the fact that medicine is complex and that doctors can't know everything at every point in time?

Is there more uncertainty, or has the uncertainty that was already in the system been revealed to us?

If doctors don't have a monopoly on access to information about medicine, how does that change our relationship with them? If doctors have constant, just-in-time access to endless amounts of information on any symptom or ailment, then how does it change what it means for them to "know"? The expression "I went to medical school to learn how to be a doctor" certainly doesn't speak to all the mandatory research that a doctor already does to maintain their license, and it definitely doesn't account for the endless amount of medical information they get on a daily basis. Their field has always been full of uncertainties; we just know more about them now. Or we think we do.

For companies like De Beers, the goal is always to make money. It's super easy to judge whether the diamond ring thing worked: Did they sell more diamonds? For more money? Did the shareholders make more money? More money! We win! That hasn't changed now that we can get information all the time and everywhere. The companies are still measuring success by making more money. We learn that we need their product for some reason or another, and they sell it to us. They have more access to information about us so they can better craft their message; but, on the other hand, we have more information coming at us, so it's a little harder to get our attention. It's a change, but not a change in goals. Their goal is still money.

We get caught in this place every time we try to learn from the corporate world. We don't have an easy way of saying what learning is for. We can't count learning (though heaven knows we try) in the same way that our friends from the corporate world get to count money. How do we know if we've made a good decision about our device use, our purchasing habits, or our voting?

In every case where our reality (what we accept as normal) interacts with information, our reality is changing. Make no mistake about it: the things that were true—the things that were commonly accepted as the things you needed to know to be ready for our society—have changed dramatically in the past thirty years. The place we go to learn something we need to learn has also changed. Maybe most important, where we go to decide what to believe has changed. The nightly news, the newspaper, a library (if we were lucky and literate enough), the people in our neighborhood: these were the limits of what we could turn to in order to decide if something was true. That has gotten more complex.

We could, if we were feeling dramatic, call it a crisis of common sense. We face a challenge in terms of knowing what should be done. Is it okay for me to send a text message at dinner? Should I stay on a social network that is run by people I morally disagree with? Is eating local more important than eating organic? What is the common sense of learning for the twenty-first century?

It is a truism to say that common sense isn't that common anymore—at least, it was a truism when I was on the phone with my father. My father would suggest that people don't have the sense that they used to have.

I think the challenge might be that we have lost our "common" more than we have lost our "sense." When my father was a child in a small town in the 1940s and 1950s, his neighbors were facing the same challenges he was. People all listened to the same music. Car tires were busted all the time. If someone listened to a show on the radio, then their neighbor was probably listening to the same show too. Party lines on telephones meant that there was no real privacy expected on the phone. The phone would ring, it was for someone on your street, and seven people answered. If it was for you, then maybe four of those other six people hung up, while the other two stayed on the line to hear what was going on. Everyone knew what they were supposed to do in those situations.

My father, who grew up without a father on the North Shore of New Brunswick, used to tell a story of shooting a deer at ten or eleven years old and bringing it to the neighbors' house so they could show him how to dress it. He gave them half of the deer in return for the lesson, and from then on, he could dress the deer on his own. He didn't need school to learn that lesson. Nor did he need it to learn how to fix a tire, or milk a cow, or run a wire for his phone to the kitchen, or change his own oil. He learned the things he needed to learn from his community.

It is the lament of every generation that the generation that follows it doesn't seem to understand the basics of practicality, good sense, or propriety. We see it at the junction of the generation that lived through World War II and the baby boomers.

We see it at the junction of those people who lived before and after World War I and the roaring twenties. These junctures occur in art, in music, and, most importantly, in the way that we live our daily lives.

Sometimes these junctions are created by the technologies that we use to support our lives. From about 1890 to about 1920, we had the invention of the car and the airplane, and the first radio news broadcast. The transcontinental telephone was first put into service in 1915. Those technologies fundamentally impacted how we could move around, what we could hear about, and how we could talk to each other. What was the commonsense way of starting a phone call in 1900? How did you decide what was true when you listened to it over the radio for the first time?

Let's zero in on that first radio news broadcast for a moment. For generations, people had been buying their newspapers from publishers that they had some sense of. They knew that the *Porcupine Gazette* or the *Daily Tombstone Epitaph* were going to have a certain perspective, based on their publishers. All of a sudden, journalists were speaking over the airwaves. Did people trust them more or less because it wasn't actually printed on paper?

We still have an echo of that in North American broadcasts in the expression "the most trusted voice in news." Where does this trust even come from?

More to the point, who is going to decide whom we're going to trust? Sometimes the decisions about how we adapt to changes in our society seem to bubble up, unstructured. Sometimes, folks like the marketer Bernays take the lead when they see an opportunity and shape how we act, often, at the risk of pointing to a theme, in order to make more money.

We as citizens are able to decide how we act in this new normal. We are responsible for passing along information that is "true," at least from a certain point of view. We are also, I think, responsible for giving children the tools they are going to need to survive in "real life." How about the tools for interpreting knowledge, for fact-checking information, or for how to work with other people?

So. I'm suggesting that we are at another one of those junctures where the reality around us has moved enough that we need to rethink what it means to know, what it means to believe something is true. We need to think about what is important to us.

When information and knowledge are hard to find, getting an answer to a problem is everything. If you discover, suddenly, the method for making a moldboard plow, then you have just doubled your ability to feed people in the surrounding region. If, three hundred years ago, you didn't know what a moldboard plow was, there was really no way for you to find out. Right now, you may just have googled that masterpiece of engineering and been really underwhelmed by the picture you saw. We now live in a world where there are fifty designer pesticides, you can buy twenty different sizes of tractors, the market for organic foods is skyrocketing, and farmers can specialize in the plant that makes up fake meat. The skill sets we require are different.

Learning in a time of abundance is different. It's different not just in the sense that we get to learn things in a new way; it's different in that the rules of engagement are different. The ways in which people are trying to trick us are different. We have new abilities we don't even know about. We have thousands—millions—of possibilities for being influenced; and we, in turn, influence the actions of others in ways we don't always see or understand. Whose right answer is it? A right answer in what context?

It's different because, for many of our challenges, there aren't solutions. Those things will always be uncertain.

Like learning itself. We can talk about learning in all kinds of ways, but the meaning of learning is always going to be one of those things that's uncertain. It's going to mean one thing in one context, and something else in another. It's going to mean something to you and something different to me. That doesn't mean we can't use the word, but it is frustrating. That uncertainty is at the core of how we need to learn in a world of information abundance. Being "certain" in many, many conversations is more a matter of belief and side-taking than it is a question of evidence.

How can I know learning is different if I can't even define it? It might be instinct of the species or it might be our training, but we want things to be clear and understandable, even when they aren't. In a world of information scarcity, you can control the definitions of things like *learning*. I think that time is gone, and we're going to have to adjust.

CHAPTER 1

Change Has Never Been a Bargain

Progress has never been a bargain. You have to pay for it. Sometimes I think there's a man who sits behind a counter and says, "All right, you can have a telephone but you lose privacy and the charm of distance." —JEROME LAWRENCE, *Inherit the Wind*

We did not invent technological disruption.

It is not unique to the early twenty-first century, and it can instill a certain amount of helplessness when we think that it is. If we are convinced that our times are unprecedented, then we have nothing to work with. None of our existing tools apply. If we're preparing for a future that we don't understand, we can pretty much do whatever we want, because who can possibly say if what we're doing is right or wrong?

There are many "thought leaders" out there right now who would like you to think that we're undergoing unprecedented change. That we're preparing for an unknown future. If their clients are convinced that we've "never seen this kind of change before," they can say whatever they want and call it "innovation." It sells a pile of books (says the guy writing a book).

Governments and the media turn to people who have had success with a particular kind of change for advice on its implications. Though just because you were the person who made money making cars doesn't mean we should ask you what the speed limit should be.

Today, the people who've made money from change are folks like the leaders of Facebook and Tesla, and we see them as people to turn to for advice on "what it all means." That's kind of like a pack of wildebeests asking a vulture about what to do about the lack of water. The argument goes like this: all these other animals are dying, and the vultures are getting fat. Those vultures must be doing something right.

Well, yes, I suppose the vultures are doing something right. They have a vested interest in the animals dying because they want to eat the animals. They are not going to come up with a plan for finding a new source of water—it's neither something they have any particular skill in nor something that they will be rewarded for doing. Quite the opposite in fact. Our Silicon Valley overlords have a vested interest in making money. Their financial success shows that they may have some expertise in making money—but that doesn't mean they can tell us how their technology impacts our lives. Or, even, how it should.

How do we adjust to the changes we are seeing around us? How does all this connection affect how we live and work together? Can we have some of these perspectives in common? Can we use our existing tools to figure all of this out?

Looking back at many periods from the Industrial Revolution until now, we see people in an uproar over how things had changed and how the new normal was much worse than what they had experienced in their childhoods. Anytime the status quo is threatened to the point where a person who used to know what was going on doesn't anymore, you've got problems. Simply put, people are frustrated by change. And if those frustrated people have any power, their feet dig in pretty quickly.

Let's talk about the telephone.

A telephone ninety years ago performed one task. A magical task. It allowed you to call someone, at a distance, and talk to them without the trouble of writing a letter or going to where they were. You could ask a question, with your voice, and get an answer right away. No waiting for a pony to run between you. I don't think it's possible for me, let alone someone who grew up with the internet, to imagine just how different that was. Imagine spending an entire day in your house without a single message from the outside world. No text. No update. No TV. Nothing.

And as Henry Drummond, the feisty lawyer in Jerome Lawrence's *Inherit the Wind*, explained, people paid for the convenience of having a telephone. Suddenly your boss could contact you at home. You could get a call from a telemarketer. From the government. Your privacy in your own house has never been the same.

The rotary phone had a dial on it that you would spin in order to connect to the person you were trying to reach. One spin for every number in a phone number. It's the mechanical version you see in old movies. It was invented in the late nineteenth century but only came into use in the 1920s. Before the rotary telephone, you would pick up your phone and tell the operator who you wanted to talk to. The limitations of this system were many, but it did have the advantage of simplicity for the user, who only had to say, "Get me Margaret."

There is a great story from the United States Senate in 1930. This was the year that technology upgrades put those nasty rotary tools of the future in every senator's office. Senators, it seems, were not happy. Some of them went so far as to propose legislation that would remove rotary telephones from their offices. They were appalled that they would somehow be expected to remember piles of multiple-digit phone numbers, each of which would connect them to a different person. I mean, who could do that? That's a secretary's job. What? You expect me to have some kind of book that holds the numbers of all the people I need to talk to? It would take forever to collect all those numbers! These guys (and they were all guys) wanted the telephone operators back. They wanted to be able to pick up the phone and tell Myrtle to find Senator Claghorn without the bother of having to remember numbers. Here's the actual text of the bill:

> Whereas dial telephones are more difficult to operate than are manual telephones; and Whereas Senators are required, since the installation of dial phones in the Capitol, to perform the duties of telephone operators in order to enjoy the benefits of telephone service; and Whereas dial telephones have failed to expedite telephone service; Therefore be it resolved that the Sergeant at Arms of the Senate is authorized and directed to order the Chesapeake and Potomac Telephone Co. to replace with manual phones within 30 days after the adoption of this resolution, all dial telephones in the Senate wing of the United States Capitol and in the Senate office building. (https://www.senate.gov/artandhistory/history/minute /Senate_Considers_Banning_Dial_Phones.htm)

I really love this example. Of particular note is "perform the duties of a telephone operator" and "failed to expedite telephone service." But one senator had more to say about it: "Senator Dill was not ready to give up. In his experience, the dial phone 'could not be more awkward than it is. One has to use both hands to dial; he must be in a position where there is good light, day or night, in order to see the number; and if he happens to turn the dial not quite far enough, then he gets a wrong connection.'"

OMG. Right? I mean, come on. You make me use two hands? And I have to use it properly for it to work? What do you want from me? That dual combination of "I am not accustomed to doing it" and "Isn't this someone else's job?" is a perfect representation of the privilege of power. It's also a response to change. That uncomfortable feeling our bodies have when contorted into an unfamiliar position to do a new task. The way we feel when we haven't yet discovered the little tricks that make a new task easier (like better lighting).

I'm not suggesting that those senators weren't busy or that it was easy in 1930 to get good lighting for your office. I mean, lighting matters, right? We do need to watch out for those responses to the new shiny thing. Sometimes those responses are something we should have. Sometimes new things are uncomfortable, and we shouldn't do them. Sometimes, though, they're uncomfortable just because we haven't taken the couple of hours required to figure them out. It's easy to look back at this example of the telephone and see a bunch of old men whining around their whiskey sours about how their privilege wasn't being respected.

The situation at the US Capitol was resolved by another senator who suggested that "younger" senators liked that they could use the dial telephone. They came up with a middle ground. Senator Tydings suggested senators be given the option of having a rotary phone or not, a solution that anyone in the technology industry will be familiar with. Let's do both instead of deciding between one or the other.

There's still so much to unpack here. First, there's the reason for the technology switch in the first place. A manual telephone is not going to "scale." It's going to work fine until you have too many people you might want to contact. I can pick up my phone right now in Ontario, Canada, and type in the fourteen-digit code of my good buddy Lawrie in the UK, and he'll pick up his cell phone (if he doesn't check the caller ID and see that it's me). Imagine trying to do that with a manual operator: "Hey, I, uh, want to talk to Lawrie. He lives in a small town near Coventry. I, uh, I think I have his address here somewhere. What? There's two of them. Oh, I, uh, I have this photo of him. Will that help?"

Connecting via an operator works fine if all you have to do is get a hold of Margaret down the hall and you have some expectation that the operator knows who Margaret is. If you have to negotiate with a person to figure out who someone is and where they might be, it's a little more complicated. I still remember doing long-distance calls with an operator, trying to find the number of a business or a person I knew but whose number I didn't have. Try to explain that to a twenty-year-old. I'll take the fourteen-digit number.

The dial telephone did not burst into usage; it was a practical solution to streamline the use of a technology. It also directly led to the loss of jobs for telephone operators. While I find it hard to believe that this was Senator Dill's concern when he was complaining about having to do the work of operators, it is unfortunately an all-too-common occurrence. The new technology replaces the work of people that we don't see.

So what have we learned from our little story of a technological upgrade in 1930?

1. Some people are uncomfortable with change.
2. Change brings uncertainty, often concerning everyday issues (in this case, lighting and having to use two hands to operate a phone).
3. People are often unwilling to do the little things that will make change easier for them.
4. People with less power in our culture (telephone operators, in this case) are often more negatively affected by change.
5. The most powerful, and often the least affected, look kind of funny eighty years later when we look back at what they did.

Of course, the new thing can actually create a need that you didn't have before. The availability of the technology creates an expectation. If you're a senator and all the other senators can reach out to their districts by punching in ten numbers, you're going to fall behind if you can't. At some point the added ease of getting a direct connection to someone is going to shift the balance.

But I would suggest that the idea that we get the technology that we need is a little too simplistic. Technological determinism. The idea that the technology we got, or the one we are getting, is the best one we could have gotten. That somehow these technologies are inevitable.

What are we (to use Henry Drummond's words) paying for the change? It's a question that we need to learn to ask ourselves so that we understand what is happening to us as we increasingly immerse ourselves in the technologies around us. If the telephone traded privacy for convenience, what about social media? How do we create a language for ourselves that lets us understand the impact of these technologies on our lives and that helps us make good decisions? We can't "decide away" Facebook any more than senators could the rotary phone. The impact of these technologies on our lives will increase, and our lives will change because of them. We *can* decide how we're going to handle that change though. I mean, not exactly Facebook, but what it represents.

In the sixty-five years following the great rotary-phone debate in the US Senate, between then and the late 1990s, our telephones slowly built up new abilities. Those abilities impacted our lives in ways that we can, maybe, understand.

Answering machines? You could have someone leave a message on your telephone when you weren't in the house. No more waiting around the house for an important phone call. You could go to the bar!

Call waiting? No more staying off the phone to make sure that an important phone call didn't hit a busy signal. You could talk to your friend for another couple of hours.

Caller ID? You could tell who was calling without the bother of picking up the phone, to the sadness of every twelve-year-old prank caller.

But these innovations took years to develop, and, importantly, each one is attached to a specific form of irritation that we can easily identify. The trade-off was not difficult to understand. The biggest thing we lost was our ability to ghost someone calling us with any degree of deniability. If, by age, you are finding that hard to follow, just pretend you're in Adele's song "Hello." "I must've called a thousand times."*

Those changes were incremental.

* "Hello" by Adele, *25*, Metropolis, 2015.

Like the rotary telephone that gave us some surety of being able to call the same person over and over again at the same number, these new innovations were all connected to practice. Don't need to stay in the house. Don't need to stay off the phone. Don't need to talk to Mom (sorry, Mom, always want to talk to you). They were commonsense solutions to problems that each person (with socioeconomic access) could relate to. And they were also common problems that were specifically exclusionary to those people without that access—people who were safely distant and without a voice, people whose exclusion was not particularly noted.

Then things started to speed up a bit. My family got a bag car phone (yup, a giant bag that was a phone) in the late eighties. It was an emergency phone, in case something happened to when we were in the woods. In the late nineties I went from a pager to a cell phone with text messaging. And then I got a cell phone with internet access. It's hard to remember now that the first iPhone was released in 2007. In a dizzying and exponential explosion, we went from text messaging and email access to the rocket-in-your-pocket power that many of us carry around now.

Your old wired phone, at least if you're old enough to have had one, lived in a world of scarcity. In 1995 we were still doing the work that the rotary phone was doing in 1920, connecting one person to another person. Each of the changes that were made to the telephone addressed simple problems with simple solutions. Those changes were incremental. The trade-offs for the new technologies were not going to fundamentally impact us the way the original telephone technology changed our lives. And even through incremental change, we still see people like our senators dig their feet in because they don't think rotary phones "expedite telephone service."

Each of those changes made it more convenient for us to communicate with another person. But that other person was, for the most part, a person we knew. There was some expectation that we would know the person calling, or at least understand the context of our not knowing. I may not know who a telemarketer is, but I can understand that they are calling from a company that is trying to sell me something that I can buy with real money.

The change that has happened to us in the last twenty or so years is more like the invention of the telephone itself. It's a transformative change. It changes our core understanding of the possibilities of how we can communicate with one another. It forces us to think about what it means to be polite, to be safe, or to be fair to one another in this new space. It forces us toward a new shared understanding of what's appropriate. A shared sense, a sense we have in common.

We have to learn a new way of doing things in our daily lives.

Our smartphones are reflective of abundance. An abundance of options, an abundance of solutions, an abundance of problems, and an abundance of exclusions. We are rapidly acquiring the need for new "commonsense" pieces to attach to that abundance, but not fast enough. Too many people are currently excluded from the conversation about what values should be driving our new perspectives, and often the people who are making the new norms are making them for reasons that might not reflect our general best interest.

Make no mistake. The change has already happened. The decisions in front of us now are more akin to those the senators faced with the rotary phone. Are we going to dig in our heels, or are we going to try to make the best of it?

And we have started developing new behaviors along with those new affordances. For example, in my circles it is mostly common practice at this point to text someone before calling them. There is an assumption of importance that comes with a direct phone call—"I feel like what I'm saying is important enough to interrupt you"—unless you are driving or a good friend and there's a reason why you'd be calling instead of texting. The new behaviors exist, but they are far from worked out.

As we dig into the practice, as we try to find the common sense, we find our values at the bottom of them. Every time you pick up your cell phone in front of your kid, what values are you passing on to your child? (This is the speech I get from my kids when I pick up my phone.)

As the apps on our phones increasingly diversify, the challenge continues and complexifies. Each app comes with potential solutions to problems that we did not think we had. They are, in many cases, problems that only exist once the apps exist. An app that gives away your location might be a good way to meet people, but it immediately creates a series of safety issues you didn't have before. You now have a problem, the app, that you need to solve. That's a long, long way from the incremental change of the "not needing to stay in the house" problem solved by the answering machine.

The technologies that power this shift really snuck up on us. Well, maybe not us, but they snuck up on me. I remember the first time I saw a Coleco version of Pong in my aunt's basement. I was young, maybe six or seven, and being in the middle of a family with a million cousins, I didn't get to play it all that often. It was mesmerizing. I can clearly remember trying to get my head around how the angles worked. I have no memory of whether I was very good at it, though I likely wanted to play more and win more than anyone else. I was that kid. It seemed like a huge deal to me at the time, but it wasn't transformative. It replicated an arcade game in your house. That's cool. But it isn't going to change your life.

We got the first computer in our house the day my parents came home with a Commodore VIC-20. It had a cassette tape drive. Uh, right. Cassette tape. There was a little plastic cartridge that had ribbon tape inside it that you put into a . . . you know what? Just google it.

It took forty-two seconds to load my favorite game, which involved a snake going through a maze and getting cut in two or something. It did not leave a big impression on me. I learned a little BASIC coding on that computer, but mostly I connected my tape drive and played games. We eventually bought a real-life desktop computer and moved into real computer land. I distinctly remember the dude from town telling us we didn't need a full 40 megabytes of hard drive space and that we should only buy 20 MB. And there was no way to connect the computer to anything or anyone outside the house.

One spring my dad broke his leg. He and my mother were lobster fishers, and so that season, I fished with her. I was nineteen. As payment, the two of them bought me a new early '90s laptop. It was huge and bulky. I opted for the black-and-white screen so I could get more RAM (computer memory) in it. I think the color screen was an extra thousand dollars or something. Those were the heady days of being able to connect to the internet with your 14.4 modem and maybe find some documents you wanted to download overnight. Fancy.

Arcade games in your house. A next-level way to type out your papers without having to use Wite-Out to fix any mistakes.

The ability to go to specific other computers with your computer to get files, assuming you knew how to do that. A place to store your files. All of these were improved ways of doing things that we were doing in an office or at an arcade. I mean, having a computer certainly meant that I could write a paper faster, but I was still just writing a paper, and I was still doing the research for it in a physical library.

That generation between the computer-type gadgets being in your house at all and them being something that could connect to the internet was an amazing leap in technological capacity. A computer you bought one year could totally be obsolete four years later. We went from talking about kilobytes to megabytes and on to gigabytes. I mean, really, who knew what a gigabyte was in 1985? But the technology didn't really have an impact on most people's day-to-day lives. People weren't getting elected or losing their jobs or buying things *because* of the technology (other than, obviously, buying the actual technology itself). I was playing games on my computer instead of on the dining room table. I could use my computer as a calculator instead of using a calculator as a calculator. I could type on a computer and print my paper out instead of using a typewriter. These were certainly improvements, but they were incremental improvements.

The real sneaking started in the late '90s. We thought, at one time, that the technology was an extension of what we were already doing. That game of Pong in my aunt's basement was just a poorer play-at-home version of what you could do in an arcade. The arcade was a fancied-up version of a pinball game. And pinball kind of feels like what you do with games at the circus, just without the benefit of cotton candy.

Technology use for learning also experienced the same kind of incremental advances. Seymour Papert was an educational technology luminary working at Massachusetts Institute of Technology starting in 1963. Papert was one of the early thinkers in educational technology, and folks still turn to him when they think about what computers mean for student learning. A visionary, he spent years thinking about how computers could help people learn to be better problem solvers. Papert had been given a set of gears by an uncle in his childhood, which he credited with starting his mind down the path to problem solving. He wanted to provide that same opportunity to learn for others, regardless of whether they had nice gear-bearing uncles. I say he wanted to advance learning rather than schools because Papert blamed the inflexibility of schools for the failure of the projects that he proposed. Let's take a look at this Papert quote from his landmark 1980 book *Mindstorms: Children, Computers, and Powerful Ideas*: "The computer is the Proteus of machines. Its essence is its universality, its power to simulate. Because it can take on a thousand forms and can serve a thousand functions, it can appeal to a thousand tastes. This book is the result of my own attempts over the past decade to turn computers into instruments flexible enough so that many children can each create for themselves something like what the gears were for me" (viii).

The computer has the power to simulate. The computer is to be like a face-to-face space. It can simulate what it is like to move gears around. It can simulate how air moves across a surface. Then, you can change the variables and try again. It can simulate things that would be too expensive or too big or too dangerous for you to have in your house or classroom.

And I get it. There are any number of things you could learn about and experience this way. You could explore procedural thinking and mathematical concepts through the exploration of things that you are fascinated by. That remains a useful thing for computers to do.

Papert also proposed a knowledge machine, a wonderful machine that could answer your questions. I mean, who doesn't want to be able to get their questions answered? What time is it? What's the date of Confederation in Canada? What are all the words to "Visions of Johanna"? Machines are good at doing this.

One example of using the "knowledge machine" that Papert proposed was a girl who wants to know how giraffes sleep. She turns to her knowledge machine, knowing that she's going to find the right answer. It's a simple question that has a verifiable answer. Papert envisioned the knowledge machine as something that children could use to explore any situation and explore it completely. Think of it like an interactive encyclopedia.

But it gets tricky. Someone has to fill that knowledge machine with answers to questions. A human, somewhere, has to go and find out if giraffes sleep lying down. And, I mean, maybe that person watched a giraffe lie down once and figured, "Yup, they sleep lying down." Maybe the information came from an exhaustive thirty-year study of giraffes that watched their every move. A quick Google search tells me that giraffes can do both.

And, frankly, I'm okay with someone filling the knowledge machine with answers to questions about a giraffe's sleeping habits. But what if the girl wants to ask the knowledge machine, "Why are some people mean?" What if we are going to ask the knowledge machine about critical race theory or whether cow's milk is healthy for humans to drink? In order for those questions to get answered, someone, or some group, has to decide what the "right" answers to those questions are.

Foundationally, that machine suggests that there are answers to questions. If I don't know something, someone else has the "answer." If I can find that knower of answers, then they can give it to me, and then I know the "answer," which, again, is fine for certain kinds of things (we might call them facts). But not all questions have those kinds of answers or even any answer at all.

You can write your secret poetry on your computer. You can use your computer to keep a record of your finances on a spreadsheet. It's yours. It lives in your house and solves the problems of having to go to an arcade, of using typewriter and Wite-Out, or of banging away at a calculator. It solves problems we knew we already had.

The internet is different. It's a transformational change. The thing it does is not like the thing it is replacing, whatever that might be.

The internet is also not the thing we asked for. If I have a horse, a faster horse is easily within the horizon of understanding to the average person. When we identify a certain thing that we lack and plan for it, make it, and then use it, there is a certain continuity. I can still ride the horse. I still need to feed it. Those early changes to the telephone, like the answering machine, changed one identifiable thing.

The internet is a tool that provides a new kind of change, with piles of unintended consequences.

Papert saw the computer as a stand-in for the gears that shaped his childhood; he thought controlling a computer would help students develop problem-solving skills. Papert also imagined a knowledge machine as a way for people to get answers. A computer and the internet can certainly be those things. They are not, however, limited to those things. The internet is not contained in a way a textbook or a gear set is.

And that lack of containment, that lack of scarcity (one question, one answer) creates a very different environment on the internet than in the world Papert imagined. If the same girl does that same search about sleeping giraffes on the internet, all kinds of things can happen. She may, for instance, find a website that is protesting poaching of giraffes. That's probably an important conversation, on the face of it, which might be important for the girl to read. Unless she's six years old. In that case, those pictures could be pretty traumatic.

The internet does not answer the question "How does a giraffe sleep?" with the answer "It sleeps lying down." I mean, it kinda does. You could certainly put that question into a search engine and get that answer. And, frankly, most of those kinds of questions will get those kinds of answers. AI-powered websites will definitely pull together some kind of answer for you. And, as a side effect, your Facebook account will start trying to sell you a giraffe piggy bank. But that's not all that is going to happen. In a world of scarcity, we have a paper encyclopedia that is sharply curated, and when you check on "giraffe," you're going to find information about the animal. You will not, however, find up-to-date information on current herd numbers. The internet is not an abundance of the information we want; it's an abundance of all information. So when we ask it more complex questions like "Why are people mean?" we can get ourselves tangled in all kinds of places. Some good. Some not so much.

Sometimes you are looking for information, for knowledge, for wisdom that is generally agreed upon. Maybe you want to decide on what dishwasher to buy. There are any number of ways to make a G chord on a guitar, but most of the websites, most of the time, are going to tell you one or two ways to do a simple one. If the first G chord you learn is the weird one I learned as a kid, it's no big deal. You can just do some more searching, do a little cross-referencing, and you'll find the normal one. Or, you know what, keep doing your weird one. No matter. You'll get a few guitar ads in your feed, but, hell, you like guitars, so that's cool.

Things get trickier when we start looking for things that don't have clear, definitive answers. Go ahead and try to figure out what it means to eat healthy or what the best kind of exercise is. Try to find the best way to heat your house. These are not questions that have actual answers. How can you best help my children prepare to be successful and happy when they grow up? There are some things you can do, and some things you probably shouldn't. But so much of it depends on context.

And what do we learn from this? In the world of a knowledge machine, we learn that things are true if they are in the knowledge machine box. Someone somewhere knows the answer to our questions, and they were kind enough to tell us. In the world of the internet, there are a thousand different answers to every question, and every answer comes connected to something else.

This internet version of knowledge is abundant and not necessarily in a good way.

CHAPTER 2

Abundance

The word *abundance* comes to us with many meanings, most of them positive. When we say that there is an abundance of something, we usually mean that there is more than enough.

I can have an abundance of paper lying around my classroom for students to use to make paper airplanes. That's good, right? Every kid gets to make their own plane, and if one kid has to try three times, no big deal. Have some more paper. Giving every kid a piece of paper to fold into a toy would have been a bit of an eye popper in a medieval European classroom. What passed as "paper" was made from scraping the skins of animals. Seriously, it took about two hundred sheepskins to make a Bible. Plus, I don't think sheepskins fly, even if you fold them the right way.

The abundance of something is hard to notice unless the idea of scarcity is still fresh enough that we remember what it was like to not have enough of something. Paper in a classroom, again, makes an interesting example. When I started as a teacher Twenty-fivish years ago, I had never heard of a quota on photocopies. I went to the photocopier, and I made copies when I needed them. In some of those early classes, we probably did more photocopied assignments than was strictly necessary. Increasingly, now, I hear of paper as a budget item. For some organizations it's an attempt at being environmentally conscious, though for others, I suspect, it's another way to cut costs. Paper in an educational environment, in some sense, is again becoming scarce. No more second paper airplane.

Our social norms in times of abundance and times of scarcity are very different. If I go to a party and someone tells me there is an abundance of snacks, I'm being told I don't really have to do a head count and make sure I only eat my share—I can eat as much as I want. It's a statement by the host that they planned for my attendance and they are able to handle the costs of creating that sense of abundance.

If there is a scarcity of food, I'm left in a very different position. I'm left with the decision of either taking advantage and eating before others or carefully choosing from the food that is available. I'm hungry, but an extra twenty people showed up to the party, so I probably don't need that second piece of pizza.

We all know that just because there is an abundance doesn't mean we *need* to take so much that we create scarcity. Not all scarcities are created equally either. We have a thousand cultural stories that talk of the kindly old couple who didn't have much in their hut but shared it all with the stranger who came to visit them in the middle of the night. Their resources were scarce, so when the old couple shared them, it was deemed more noble.

Scarcity and abundance require us to think differently about the ways in which we interact with the people around us. For those of us fortunate enough to be able to afford the electricity in our houses, we've not had to worry about how much energy there is. Flick the switch. The light turns on. An endless stream of energy comes in through the power lines to our houses. We burn energy continually in our cars. There is an abundance of power available, so using it to power a watercooler in my house is not a big deal. I can afford it, but should I do it?

It depends on whether I think the energy is scarce or abundant. Am I just looking at the power coming into my house, or am I looking at the whole system? If I think of that watercooler as something I'm doing with abundant energy, it's just a question of paying the extra money on my power bill. If I think of it as part of the system, that watercooler becomes an extra draw on a potentially scarce international energy reserve.

The examples of the snacks and the watercooler represent material abundance. We might argue about what constitutes an abundance of snacks or whether there are scarce energy reserves, but, regardless, they are material. That abundance of limited material goods comes at a cost. When we look at the total context in which that abundance sits, we can see that our usage of energy in an "abundant" way leads to increased pressure on the climate (a complex system) and catastrophic impacts on our planet. Over the centuries we have moved from a scarcity interaction to an abundance framework as we relate to energy, and we are starting to pay for it with melting ice and increased storms.

Our ways of thinking about material abundance as personal or systemic has a profound impact on how we see the world. But those are things that we can readily point to and see—things that are used and then gone, or at least changed. In his 1974 think piece "As Far as Eye Can See: Knowledge Abundance in an Environment of Scarcity," Glen Eye draws the distinction between an abundance of things that have a limited quantity, say oil, and an abundance of something like information.

An abundance of information—something that is not limited by how many times we use it—is a totally different bag of potatoes. A website viewed one million times might make an extra draw on a server somewhere, but it won't have anywhere near the same impact on a forest as making a million books out of trees will, or, to look back a little further in time, the same impact on sheep as making a million books out of sheepskins.

How is this kind of abundance a problem to anyone? Shouldn't it be good that we have more information available to us? Living in a world of information scarcity meant that you might not be able to find the things you wanted or that you might have to travel to another town to find it. It turns out we've been at this intersection of the technology we have and the way it impacts how and what we learn for a long time.

> "Those who wish to scrutinize the bosom of nature to the inmost can hear the books of Aristotle which were forbidden at Paris."
> —University of Toulouse advertisement posted at the University of Paris in 1270

In this book, the specific kind of abundance I'm talking about is an abundance of information. Compare our current situation to the impact of the printing press. We went from it taking the deaths of sheep and a poor bored monk writing by hand by candlelight to make a book to being able to run off hundreds of copies of a book (identical books) in one shot. That profoundly changed how information could be disseminated. Books were more accurate (or at least, they had the same mistakes) when run off a printing press. The cost in human hours was also reduced. But it was still a trade-off. We lost the art of crafting a book by hand. When you spend months or years drawing something by hand, it is more personal, more individual, and sometimes, more beautiful. You could certainly have more books with a printing press, but you're going to be less selective about the ones you decide to make.

Of course, the advent of the printing press didn't lead to everybody suddenly reading their way to success or publishing their way to authority. In a world where there was hardly anything to read, there was little need for literacy. Most people couldn't read and had no reason to believe the things they needed to know would be in a book. This last piece feels important. We'll never know how the average nonreader felt about books (they, you know, didn't write books), but you've got to wonder what use they would have found in one.

The person who did want to learn from dusty old tomes at a university in 1270, quoted in the flyer above, wanted to "hear" the words of Aristotle. We lost poor Aristotle about 1,600 years before the University of Toulouse existed, so there's no need to imagine him chained to a lectern attracting students. When we read, not only are we listening as a learning process, but we're also listening to someone who is no longer with us. You can imagine the reader in front of the class reading aloud from the book so that all the students could "hear" the books of Aristotle. (*Physics*, in this case, was the one that was banned in Paris.)

Learning was listening. You could certainly ask questions, and argumentation was part of that university structure, but it wasn't exactly easy to get your grimy paws on that book. Better for you to sit back and try to remember what Aristotle said.

That printing press—it was transformational. It meant that if you could afford it, you could get your hands on the book and read it for yourself.

But it would take projects like the one Johann Pestalozzi took on in Switzerland around 1800 to bring "reading for knowledge" to the masses. He had a dream that he would teach the whole of Switzerland to read. His book *How Gertrude Teaches Her Children* is an amazing glimpse into the challenges of teaching things using books in a time of information scarcity. His attempt to bring textual literacy to the whole of Switzerland happened over three hundred and fifty years after the invention of the printing press. The work that Webster did bringing textbooks to the masses in the 1840s in America happened almost four hundred years after Gutenberg. It took a *long* time for us to adapt to the different literacies we would need to go along with the technology of printing.

But it did happen. We adapted. The abundance set in. All those papers and books were filling up libraries and bookstores, and there was no way to have all the books or know all the things. People could read them, but there were too many for any one person to read. We were already moving from scarcity to abundance. But it was an abundance for experts in a given field, not an abundance for regular people in their regular lives.

Our more recent transformational change in information abundance has happened on a shorter timeline. When I was in high school, the web did not exist. I learned to type on a mechanical typewriter (never knowing how critical that skill would become in my future career adventures). I learned to do research in a physical library and learned the lyrics to songs by listening to them over and over again. I talked to my girlfriend on a telephone that I was sharing with the other people in my parents' house. We had a set of encyclopedias, the *Encyclopedia Britannica*, in our living room that we would pull down when we wanted to know the answer to something.

Here I am at forty-nine years old, over thirty years later, and most of my career has been built on how I use the web and who I've met through using it. In four hundred years a society has, maybe, the time to adjust its values so that a person knows how to deal with the shift to information abundance, though our friend Glen Eye quoted earlier would suggest that abundance only set in in the mid to late twentieth century.

We've had twenty-five years to adapt to the internet. The shift I'm talking about, though, is not mostly a technological one. Certainly, the technological structure of the internet works in ways that lead us down certain paths. The same way that the printing press encouraged people to write long pieces for efficiency, the internet's low bar for creation encourages us to make more, faster and shorter. I may be typing these words on a computer, but the words themselves are still the same ones that I would have typed during Mrs. Degrace's tenth-grade typing class. The telephone in my pocket still allows me to talk to people on the other side of the world, just like the one on the wall of my parents' kitchen did, although it is less expensive to make a long-distance call now. But my phone also doubles as a computer that allows me to connect to the internet and, through it, to billions of other people, twenty-four hours a day.

When Eye talked of "abundance" in 1974, he was suggesting that all the information about something was more than one person could remember if that person was out there looking for it. That abundance has come home. And it's multiplied. There are any number of dramatic stats out there that attempt to measure how much, but let's just agree that it's *a lot*. Eye was tracking a slow, incremental change to abundance. What we're talking about here is a transformational change.

The simple fact is, we don't really know what we're supposed to do at the information abundance party. I can hear the words "I need to get better at sorting the data and not remembering the data," but what does that mean for me on a day-to-day basis? Does it mean that being good at trivia doesn't make me smart anymore?

And it's not just the quantity that's changed. The "quality" has also changed. Eye was talking about more of the same kind of thing. We now have more information of many different kinds. A lot of the information that we consume is being created by other people like you and me. We're making comments on social media posts. It's being created by AI systems that generate their own content based on what it learns from the web. We're leaving reviews on Google for the restaurant we visited. We might have taken a video of our bread baking. We are, all of us, part of creating the abundance of information.

Here's the problem. We were not trained for a world that had too much information; we were trained for a world that had too little information. Our ways of thinking about the world have prepared us for the scarcity party.

We are the nouveau riche of the information management set. We have all the wealth and none of the aplomb.

The big difference, of course, is that there is no "old riche." Or, maybe, they do exist, and they are the purveyors of knowledge that we used to have who understand information by different rules. Religious leaders in our communities. Your mom. That loud guy at the end of the bar. We have no one to turn to, to help us decide what we should be doing now that we've moved from information scarcity to information abundance. You could see that as an advantage, as we've got a pretty clean slate with regards to what we do with that abundance.

You could.

What do I mean by *information* and *knowledge* you say? I could give you a dictionary definition or pick from a researched article or a magazine or a Facebook post—they'd all say something different. One of the key skills I think we need to bring to the information abundance party is being able to find ways to explain to people what we mean by a word in a given context. Appealing to one authority, or thinking there is one place that can tell you what something is, is just that; it's an appeal to authority. And that can still work. Some things are material-type things in the world. And some things, like the difference between information and knowledge, are just things we need to negotiate. You don't need to agree with my distinction; you just need to know what I mean by it so you can follow what I'm trying to say.

Think of it this way. You're walking down the street and between your senses and your phone you pick up tons of information. You get the names of streets, the menus for restaurants, and a little plaque that tells you who was in this very place two hundred years ago. You might have some knowledge too. Let's say your uncle Eddy told you to go to the potato restaurant on the corner because they make the best baked potato ever. Now you know your uncle Eddy, and you can decide how much to trust that knowledge you have—you might even use some of the information available. Maybe the restaurant is packed, and you can smell it from here and it smells awesome. Maybe you know your uncle Eddy has terrible taste in potatoes. Information is the raw material you have to work with. Knowledge is that information put in a package by a person or a process.

Does that make it clearer? Maybe not. I worry about getting bogged down in this distinction. I understand that can be frustrating. Suffice it to say that information could be facts or data, and knowledge could be wisdom, or processed information.

We have an absolute abundance of information, meaning we have way more things we need to process, and the ways we used to do that are not all fit for our purposes.

Ten years ago, my family was hiking in the woods with another family and our then three-year-old broke free from the hand she was holding and sprinted off into the woods. By the time I got my hands on her, she had fired a handful of random berries into her mouth. I froze for a second, then dug the ones she hadn't swallowed out of her mouth and took a picture of those berries before running for home.

Five hundred years ago, if you wanted to know what those berries were, you would have had to find someone nearby who could tell you about them. My father knew them as "the berries you shouldn't eat." I could have gone to the library to find them in a book I suppose, but I popped the picture on Twitter before jumping in the car and heading to the hospital.

We got two IDs on the picture from friends on Twitter long before poison control called us back. (We called them, too.) One of those fine people actually sent us the first aid recommendations for the berries (baneberry), which we forwarded to the hospital. That information probably saved our daughter a stomach pumping that day.

The process of coming to know is different.

You could say that the abundance of information gets in the way of us processing our way to knowledge. When there's so much information flying at us, we can't take the time to do the processing work to help us make good decisions. There is also an abundance of folks who are most willing to "help" you with your decisions. They do the translation of information to knowledge and give you the end result. That can be an enormous relief. And it can also be dangerous.

For some, figuring out the "information" of song lyrics was a right of passage. It certainly was for me. I still remember the moment, in 1992, when my friend from university turned to me and shouted, "Bone to be chewed!" It was the lyric in the middle of "The Wreck of the Edmund Fitzgerald" that we had been trying to figure out for months.* I just confirmed that information with a five-second Google search for "Wreck of the Edmund Fitzgerald lyrics." That's a simple example and one that is endlessly entertaining to my sixteen-year-old child. Young people can't see it. They think it's funny that it took us so long to figure things out, but they have always read the lyrics along with any new song that they've sung. For them, lyrics are available. Does that mean they understand the song better? Well, knowing what the words are certainly helps, but thinking about the song and the sailors that died in the November gale that came early is probably the same in both cases.

There are lots of ways in which this abundance affects our daily lives. Grandma's recipe book rarely hits the counter anymore, as I have access to thousands of versions of any recipe that I might want to make. I have taught myself some fairly rugged carpentry by watching YouTube videos and Instructables. When I hear a song in the grocery store that I like and don't know the name of, I pull out my phone and capture the song and listen to it later. Each of these examples represents a small improvement

* "Wreck of the Edmund Fitzgerald" by Gordon Lightfoot, *Summertime Dream*, Reprise Records, 1976.

in our quality of life, certainly one we could live without but one that still makes our lives more enjoyable. Each of them gives us a little glimpse into how abundance changes what it means for us to "know" and how we go about knowing.

The recipe example is probably the one closest to my heart. I love to cook. My mother is an excellent cook. The things she cooks she cooks well, but I can't really turn to her when I want to be able to cook something different. We have a beautiful handwritten cookbook from my partner's great-aunt that is one of our family's treasures. Anytime someone wants to make a delicious dessert from the '50s, that's the place to turn to. I heartily advise pineapple cream. It's basically whipped cream and canned pineapple. And it's delicious.

When I wanted to learn how to make fresh pasta with the kiddos, however, I had to turn to the internet. I have no Italian grandmothers at my disposal to walk me through the process. I started reading the arguments about how much egg yolk belongs in the mix and how long to let it dry and how long to mix it. Like many searches, there was core information about the topic, which deviated only slightly, the "Yeah, whatever, this will probably be close enough" response. There was a set of search results from boutique or curated websites that gave the inside scoop on how to get it done just right. And there was another set of websites that gave dumb advice because they were just trying to sell something. Or would have downloaded a virus if I even visited their websites.

Picking up the phone to call my mom and ask her a question is a literacy that I have deep in my bones. I have a mother who gets off the phone if she gets any hint that I might be busy with something. It's a real blessing. I know how to call her, but it isn't going to get my pasta made. Indeed, my mother, at this point, will tell me to "ask googles." The great-aunt's recipe book is limited to the things she wrote in it so many years ago. It will not grow with new recipes. There is scarcity in both situations, the scarcity of my mother's and my cooking experiences and the scarcity of what one nice little old lady was able to write in a spiral-bound scribbler two generations ago.

The internet recipes, however, are abundant. I have way *more* choices than I need. I can choose between the riskier version or the safe version. I need to keep my wits about me to avoid going to websites that are going to harm my computer. If I'm going with a safe choice, I need to choose between those options, maybe based on the rating that the website has or a comment that someone else has left with the recipe. On some pages I have to scroll past twenty-seven ads and the entire life story of the recipe before I actually get to the recipe. If I'm using a serious cooking website (I'm looking at you, serious eats.com), then I'm trusting my own relationship with the website that I've developed on previous occasions. What I get from that website will probably be good enough. There are a lot of variables.

I mean, getting access to all these things is a win, right? I can get access to way more things than I could before. The food in my house is better. I'm learning new things.

But there are things that we lose at the same time. Time spent in the kitchen with the little old man who bakes bread or the mother learning how to cook are cultural connections we've always had. If I hadn't been able to find out how to make pasta, maybe I would've made an effort to get to know the nice Italian lady around the corner and asked her to teach me how to make it. Of course, just because she's Italian doesn't mean she makes pasta, but you get what I mean.

Maybe we don't need the skills to reach out and meet people in the same way we did before, but that sure seems like a loss to me. If we don't have to turn to the people in our lives but can just search the internet instead, do we lose a piece of our culture? We lose some of the in-between skills that are involved in communicating with one another. There are so many hidden trade-offs for abundance.

Think about the random conversations people used to have while standing in line or sitting on a bus—"laughing on the bus, playing games with the faces."* (Thanks, Paul Simon.) There is a power to boredom. Before we all had phones at our fingertips, boredom was something that we had around us all the time. Now boredom is a choice you have to make.

There is a value to constraints.

Talk about a twenty-first-century literacy. How do we constrain access to information in order to allow people to learn more broadly? How do we learn deeply when there is so much going on? And we're still talking about things that are low stakes. I mean, bad pasta is still pasta. Add sauce and cheese, and it's going to be awesome.

How do we stop having fun with all the things that are served to us and learn anything at all? Whether your thing is TikTok or YouTube videos of people fixing guitars or the world news, you never really need to be short of entertainment.

Figuring out how we can adapt to all this abundance is, I think, a learning problem. Learning in an era of information scarcity (every era up until twenty or so years ago) and learning in an age of information abundance are bound to be different processes. I'm not just talking about "the way we learn stuff

* "America" by Simon and Garfunkel, *Bookends*, Columbia Records, 1968.

in schools," though that's a part of it. We certainly take that version of learning with us through the rest of our lives. There are other less formal versions of learning that we do everyday. We cook. We vote. We raise children. We adapt to new realities.

The folks confronted with the printing press got a few hundred years to figure this out. So far, we've had twenty.

CHAPTER 3

How Abundance Is a Problem for Learning

The internet gives me information abundance. I can find recipes. I can find out what the capital of New Zealand is (it's not Auckland). I can call people around the world for free. And you, Dave, can find out what the lyrics were to all the songs from your childhood. I'm not seeing the problem.

Well, the problem is that some things, and many of the most important things, don't respond well to a search engine. If we were really using Papert's knowledge machine, then there'd be much less of a problem. If we could trust one central "Knowledge Research Team" somewhere to give us the answer to every question, we'd be fine. Alternately, if there were only one thing that we had to understand deeply, let's say "the way to enrich soil so that our garden continues to grow year after year," we could accumulate the facts, the experiences, and the knowledge for doing that one thing.

But it's not one thing. It's *all the things*.

We not only have instant access to minute-by-minute news sites telling us what's happening all over the world, an abundance overload on its own, but we also have social messaging coming in through our variety of connections. Without even realizing it, we are suddenly a part of hundreds of other conversations we don't have the background to make good decisions about. Scientific issues like climate change, virus management, and wildlife conservation are coming at us, with all the corporate influences, the bad actors, and the blowhards included.

And then, people do "the research." They spend (let's be generous) a couple of hours googling information and then decide what to believe. They might be researching the purchase of a new dishwasher or a bicycle or their ancestors in a library. We all do this "research" all the time.

That is not the same thing, however, as what researchers mean by the word *research*. Researchers would call the dishwasher thing something like "reading" or, at best, "searching." Research, as it is used by professional researchers, is a massive undertaking. As a professional researcher, you first need to spend years getting a sense of how a given field works. You then need to choose a research process and understand that process well enough to explain it to someone else. Then, you can use your research method to build a very small amount on the vast amount of work that's already been done. That takes years. Years before you can even start to write. You can rarely (if at all) "do your own research" in someone else's area of expertise.

Research can take on very different meanings. If you hear a sports figure say "they've done their own research," they probably mean the dishwasher kind of research, not the researcher kind of research. Don't get me wrong, dishwasher-style research is still important. But the stakes aren't very high, and you are directly involved because you need a dishwasher. The research you are going to be reading is also already customized for you, the dishwasher purchaser, to read. You are (unless you are a very special person) not going to be reading about the compliance of the rubber seals or which alloy they use in the construction of the dishwasher tubs. The dishwasher research you can do is designed for you. The company is directly marketing to you and other people with interests similar to yours.

The other kind of research has an entire language that you are precisely *not* the target for. It has often long, confusing words with very precise meanings that are a shorthand for the people who are in that field. It used to be hidden from you. I mean, not on purpose. It existed. There was data about the failure rates of certain medicines, and there were random people who thought that we were all being poisoned by random things in our environment. There were conspiracies. We just couldn't see them. That information was difficult to find, and if you found it, you only found one version of it. It was a voice in the wilderness. It wasn't connected. It wasn't abundant. It was scarce.

Now, we can see every conversation. Get access to every controversy. Listen in on the thoughts of every dishwasher-style researcher who has thoughts about our health. We hear all the voices and perspectives that are out there. And, sadly, we've been taught that to be "smart," we need to have "an opinion on it."

That's a lot of decision making to take on.

I have a standing rule when I manage projects to try to never ask anyone for an opinion about something they aren't likely to know something about. I have noticed, over the years, that people without a background in a given topic are more likely to take up rigid positions. The more you know, the more you see the uncertainty. The less you know, the more many of these complex situations seem like just a matter of taking sides.

There's a great Saturday Night Live skit about this. It's set up like a version of Jeopardy, except the game is called "Should I chime in on this?" The game is simple. When asked for an opinion in an area where you don't have personal experience or expertise, you just say, "No, I shouldn't chime in on that." Contestants are asked their opinions about the Syrian refugee crisis, and the correct answer for these contestants is supposed to be "No, I shouldn't chime in on that." As you can imagine, no one wins. Everyone chimes in. On everything.

When confronted with a complex idea, like the Syrian refugee crisis, that many of us don't have the context to comment on, we tend to take a position based on the information we do have, which for many of us is not very much. We want to be able to sound smart. I mean, someone has asked us the question, so shouldn't we have an answer for it? We ignore or simply don't understand the complexity of the situation to be able to participate in the conversation.

Lacking the knowledge to maintain uncertainty, we default to certainty.

And if we don't know, a quick Google search will fix it, right? I mean, if I can find the capital of New Zealand, I can learn what I need to know to decide how I feel about the fuel economy of my new car, right? We're smart.

Let's assume that you and I are fine. We've got it sorted. Let's imagine someone else who doesn't have the time to be as well-informed as we are. Can they understand the difference between a simple question (one that has a factual answer) and a complex question (one that has many, many different answers and varying points of view that could be equally valid)?

That is the critical point that we need to understand to be able to address all this abundance. Some things are factual;

there is general agreement amongst people on what the answer to the question is. I used to work in a lead and silver refinery. I can tell you, right now, that lead melts at 327.5 degrees Celsius. There's no debate. It does it every time. It's irrelevant that I used to work in a refinery. My "authority" here is not an issue.

But that is, often, what we're looking for: a reason for trust. I'm claiming a reason for trust by stating that I used to work in a refinery, but my employment history has no impact on the temperature at which lead melts. The truth is that I had to check.

Let's use an everyday challenge that doesn't have an answer but is something that happens in real life: Should I encourage my daughter to play soccer?

There's our question. Not *should* she, but *should I encourage her.* Some random thoughts and googling lead me to the following positions:

1. She's not a huge fan of team sports, though she seems to do fine working with groups in her theater troupes.
2. She already goes to karate, but more exercise is better.
3. Girls get concussions almost three times more often than boys in high school soccer.
4. Rates of high school girls getting concussions are almost as high as high school (American) football rates.
5. I think she secretly likes soccer.
6. Team sports can make for good relationships and help develop collaborative skills in ways that other solo activities can't.
7. Concussions are bad. Way worse than we used to think they were.

This is what real-life decisions often look like. We have a bunch of random thoughts, beliefs, and facts, and we need to work through them to come to a decision. Let's take a look at each point. It's important to note, though, that while I can't be guaranteed that most of these positions are "correct," they are what I have to work with.

1. Her team sports experience is just, like, my opinion man.
2. I drive her to karate. I know that's happening.
3. I found the concussion facts in a *Forbes* article that cited a *Pediatrics* journal article I don't have access to.
4. Same.
5. Opinion.
6. Generally accepted cultural comment that I have some doubts about.
7. I've heard an awful lot about concussions being bad related to things like professional football and just take it for granted.

So, how do I choose? I mean, team sports are good, right? And exercise is important. But she hasn't specifically brought up soccer, and do I want to encourage her to play soccer only to have her get a concussion?

Given this collection of random thoughts, I've made the decision that I'm not going to encourage her to start playing soccer. The risks of concussions seem to be approaching some level of scientific consensus, and those risks can have a serious impact on her quality of life as she gets older.

This conversation changes, maybe, if she comes to me directly and asks to play. But this is real life. We are constantly confronted with complex decisions. It could be voting. It could be our purchasing habits and their impact on climate change. Before the internet, I would not have gotten that specific concussion information easily, if at all, and it's that "fact" that impacts my decision making. Those "facts" are *everywhere*, and they impact our lives, our decisions, and the world that we live in. So much so that it's tempting to ignore some and just pick the ones that best suit our own perspectives. So how can we decide what and who we are going to trust? How do we use all of this abundance to make good decisions?

Like in this case, I don't happen to like some of the facts. I grew up playing soccer. My brother played. My sister played. My eldest child played for a while. I kind of like soccer. And now I have the pesky facts telling me that it might be dangerous to play.

Abundance being what it is, I could find other facts—facts that say what I want them to say.

We have always been in a bit of a bind when it comes to reliability and the internet. Most of the information you can find in books is now available online. But when those same authors who wrote those books write something digitally, it is somehow now less trustworthy. It hasn't had the magic book-binding sauce of truth.

And, frankly, there is kind of a magic book-binding sauce. It takes a long time to publish a book. It costs a lot of different people money. Those factors will reduce the number of people sharing their information. That makes it harder for someone who is just causing trouble to justify creating disinformation. It also means that many voices that can't afford the time and money won't be heard on any given issue. And, of course, something being hard doesn't make it true.

Somewhere at the forefront of the debate over online reliability, for the past twenty years anyway, has been Wikipedia. Should it be used as a reference in a paper? ("No!" I hear you shout.) Even some of the people who started the website agree with you. The website "Wikipedia" was originally just a testing site for the "real" project that the company was working on called "Nupedia." (Spoiler alert: Nupedia didn't amount to much, but Wikipedia stuck around.)

The original plan from the founders of Wikipedia was that experts were going to volunteer their time to create articles on everything, and we'd end up with something that looked like an internet version of an encyclopedia. (Sound familiar? That's our knowledge machine again.) They tried to use the internet as a publishing platform for content, and what they got was a community-created website for the world's information. A website that followed a totally different set of rules.

And that is the point.

An information website that is updated constantly is not the same thing as a book. It has correct information or wrong information for different reasons. Does Wikipedia have more wrong information than my 1970s *Encyclopedia Britannica*? It probably does simply because it has more information overall. But it is often going to be more correct in terms of time. The information in the encyclopedia is going to have all the advantages of it being difficult to publish on paper.

A book that is printed on paper starts to drift toward wrong the second it leaves the editing room. I mean, it may have all kinds of different wrong things in it before it gets edited; but once published, it is instantly out-of-date. Like a car driven off the lot of a car dealership, it loses its value as it ages.

We're not talking about books as art or literature. We're talking about our knowledge being reliable. Art is a whole other bag of potatoes.

We have other words for "reliable" when it comes to paper books though. We know that a book that was published in, say, 2002, is not one we should necessarily take advice from when fixing our computer. That book might have been useful in 2003, maybe even 2004. There might be small parts of it that are still useful now, but you'd need to be an expert to tell the difference. You'd need to already know enough about computers that you wouldn't need the book anyway.

In school, we were taught to look at things like the publisher, the year of publication, and then maybe a recommendation from a friend or a librarian. You bought the book. You hoped for the best.

That, my friends, is not much to go on. But, unless you were magically an expert in the field you were trying to understand, what else were you going to do?

But it's what we had. You might get a newspaper on your doorstep. You could watch the news or listen to the radio and get the information someone else decided you might want. You might get a magazine delivered once a month or pick one up at the corner store. But getting something like a book was hard work twenty-five years ago. I mean, getting a specific book on a specific topic. Sure, if you worked at a university or lived down the street from a world-class library, maybe it wasn't *that* hard; but, for most of us, getting information was hard.

Well, now it isn't.

And it's easy to forget that we're only fifteen years into the portable cell-phone-as-internet revolution. We're only twenty or so years into the average person having an internet connection.

That is not a lot of time to update our tools for evaluating the truth of something we're reading. The "our" in that sentence is super relevant. I'm not suggesting that researchers have started evaluating their research differently. I'm not saying that journalism is evaluating truth differently (though it has certainly shifted in other ways). I'm suggesting that the day-to-day work that each of us does to make decisions has changed.

This is a crisis of the everyday.

It's a problem for nonspecialists. We've all been taught, one way or another, how to think about writing or reading or figuring things out. For many of us . . . ahem . . . that time we were taught was a long time ago. But I do mean "nonspecialist" not "uneducated." I've taken probably fifteen math courses in my life, maybe more. I recently taught ninth grade math to my teenager. I'm not "uneducated," but I'm certainly not a specialist.

The decisions we make every day are important. We're being asked to vote on things. We're buying things. We're posting our feelings online, all of which, together, have a massive influence on our society. We need to be able to make good decisions.

Our skills, though, they're from a different time. The people who figured out how to judge the value of a paper document took years and years to figure out what to do and how to spread that information around. We need to do the same evaluation on how we get information digitally.

Let's look a little deeper at the Wikipedia example.

Anyone can edit it—even a nonspecialist like me—so the information there must be garbage. That's the most common criticism I've heard about it.

While it is true that anyone can get an account on Wikipedia and anyone can edit a page, the actual process of editing is a bit more involved than that. For instance, rules around current events can be quite wide open. As new information comes in, the content is checked by editors. If it's a page of a well-known person, it's going to be watched more closely.

We're willing to accept an old book being wrong because it's out-of-date. But we don't like Wikipedia *because* it can be updated.

If you understand what Wikipedia *is*, then it can be an excellent information tool. The entry on concussions that I used to start my research on girls' soccer includes some anecdotal soccer concussion stories and also some links to formal research. It is a super effective part of the information landscape because it is connected to other pages. Connected to other locales of trust. It doesn't make the information accurate, but it does mean that you know what to expect when you go to that website. It's part of a bigger process of helping us make good decisions.

I'm afraid to say that one of the answers to all of this is that you can't look to only one place *for any* important information. It's always a process of "coming to know." I mean, that's partially because there's so much to know, and in many circumstances, we aren't going to have the background to find information that is going to help us make good decisions.

When information was scarce, it was easier to think that the decisions we were making were based on "perfect" information. By the time the information had reached us, it had been through a researcher and then a reporter and then maybe someone who heard that reporter once. Now, we can see the research itself (note that I said "see" and not "understand"; most of us will never be able to fully understand the research), and we can see the opinions of dozens of other people about it, people whose understanding of that research varies.

It's also because people are specifically and purposefully trying to fool us.

Take the story of "fake news."

One of the first uses of the term *fake news*, as far as I can tell, was by Canadian journalist Craig Silverman in a tweet about purposeful disinformation appearing in news stories. His research went on to track what seemed like a concerted effort to create news that was purposefully false but also intended to draw attention to itself due to its dramatic nature.

The town of Veles in Macedonia is an interesting case in point. In what likely sounds like a plot for a Hollywood movie, a small town in Macedonia started working on creating fake news stories to generate ad revenue online. Whether it was the threat of low bacon reserves or any of the hundreds of fake political stories, they attracted people's attention. People clicked on the links. The people who wrote the fake news got money for those clicks. It worked. The people making the stories made a lot of money.

They didn't necessarily care what the story was. They designed the stories to go viral, regardless of the content.

But with what outcome? Some people see a story and are shocked by it. Others might find that the same story matches their own secret suspicions about the lack of bacon, and they share it. This "disinformation" becomes "misinformation." It goes from someone writing something they know is false to someone sharing it not knowing it's false. It gains speed. It spreads.

The term *fake news* continued to grow and morph as it became an expression used in the 2016 Trump campaign. In that context, it started to take on a different tone. It was no longer news that was *actually* fake in the sense that it was totally made up by cynical folks who were trying to make a living. It was "fake" in the sense that the person who was hearing the story didn't agree with or like the story.

"That's fake news," as we now say it, might mean that the speaker sees the story as biased or flawed in some way. That transition from one to the other happened in a couple of years' time. And, further, the phrase "that's fake news" now gets used to mean that we don't like what a person has said.

This is what abundance looks like in the wild. The term *fake news* is reasonably new. It has numerous meanings to different people. In some sense, it depends on the context, and if you missed it, culturally, it takes a long time to get your mind around what is going on. That's one example of one concept. Understanding the story of fake news is like understanding what's happened to us, and it can give us a path toward understanding what we can do about it.

We need to understand, first and foremost, that the folks in Macedonia didn't necessarily care how they were impacting people. Their news stories about conspiracy theories in the United States were designed for clicks. Anyone clicking through one of the stories and ending up on the website makes them a small amount of money. When there are millions of people clicking, it starts to add up.

This means the more the story gets shared, the more people circulate the story (even if they circulate it in jest), and the bigger the chance that the story will get clicked on. More clicks mean more advertising revenue. As professional disinformation people, like those in Veles, started to understand that the factionalism in different parts of the world was as strong as it was, they began to feed it. They began to write increasingly dramatic and outlandish stories that appealed to people's beliefs that the other side of the political spectrum was not to be trusted.

So, people in a small town in a foreign country write ridiculous news stories on made-up news sites and affect a foreign election. And they do it with no particular interest in what happens in the election but only because they can make money in the process. That is abundance. It's not that people haven't written outright lies on paper and published it before. It's that no one could have ever written hundreds of stories on paper from a small town in southeastern Europe and spread them across millions of households throughout the world. It's the scale that's changed.

This exploitation exposed the hidden safety net of paper that we never even realized was there. Just the cost of paper and postage has stopped us from being able to do this before. One of the neat things about old Roman ruins (made particularly obvious in a city like Pompeii that was buried under volcano dust for 1,600 years) is just how much electioneering materials are found scribbled onto the walls. "Elect Servius, he bakes great bread!" But there are only so many walls and so many people walking by to read them.

When the printing press started coming on in the sixteenth century, people created political pamphlets; they were effective, but you had to really want to get something out there to go through the expense and the effort of getting your brand of lies printed on paper. And how many copies are you going to print? A hundred? A thousand?

The restriction of the cost of paper is *a huge* help to your dishwasher-style research skills. If there is a strict limit to the number of people who can afford to create information, that makes your research much easier. It also limits the reasons why someone would create and disseminate disinformation to try and trick you. And, ultimately, it means that there's less misinformation being passed around by people who never check the information they hear. Bad information still exists. Just less of it.

Imagine the effort involved in trying to publish a paper-based history of my hometown in northern New Brunswick that included an eleventh-century Danish castle on the coast somewhere. We could make up a story about how there was a second boat that carried on from L'Anse aux Meadows, Newfoundland to the coast and set up a kingdom. What's the market for that kind of book? Traditional paper publishers wouldn't touch it because there's no way to recoup the investment needed to publish it. You'd need to create your own publishing company. Then, how would you get it into bookshops without a distributor? How would the dozen potential buyers ever even hear about it?

It would take me twenty minutes to build a website about my castle, and it would cost me next to nothing.

Right now, millions upon millions of people are using the internet to get their message across, from old publishing companies and established news outlets to advertorials from companies and bad actors from all political stripes trying to convince us of something. And, also, just bad actors. People who do it for the simple joy of taking power over someone else. For the LOLs. With the new generative AI tools, this process is just going to get easier and easier. You won't even need to really understand the language you are creating content in. Ask something like ChatGPT to write you a disinformation story, wait fifteen seconds, and you're done.

Every time one of those news items gets taken up as a fact, it has an impact on our decision making. Think about the soccer example from earlier. High school girls are at a high risk of getting concussions. The core fact in the middle of all that thinking is the deciding factor. That piece of information seems to be true. If you can make people believe certain kinds of facts, it can have a profound impact on our decision making and, ultimately, our culture.

If a made-up fact is that our security services are not to be trusted or that vaccinations are not worth it, then that decision making starts to get messy. Think about vaccination. It is accepted medical practice to vaccinate. Millions of people used to get sick and die who don't now because we vaccinate people. One article comes out twenty years ago in a respected publication (long since withdrawn) with some cooked-up data in it, and suddenly people are doubtful about vaccinations.

And, worse, they are suspicious of science.

Once the virus of a made-up fact starts to spread, it can be difficult to control. This is the other side of our ability to find any information. We can find *any* information, whether it's true or not. Because there are no controls on the veracity of information or the means to disseminate it, our version of Papert's knowledge machine won't give you a straight answer.

This abundance of information is not just something we are receiving; it's something we are part of. There is an abundance of voices out there that you can listen to and communicate with. That shift has profound effects on what it means to know and, we've been arguing, requires some pretty serious rewiring as to how we think about learning and knowledge.

In an environment of information scarcity, the things we say and do burn off into the air. I can sit in my house and yell at the TV because my least favorite sportsball player has made a mistake, and the worst that happens is that I scare the cat. Now, with a quick flurry of a finger, I can @ that player on Twitter and start a campaign to end their career.

A regular person can have more impact on the world than at any other time in history, and it isn't even close.

In our personal lives, casual mean comments used to burn off into our cars. You get invited to a friend's house for dinner, and what would once have been a nasty comment to your partner on the drive home, "That dinner was terrible. Who even does that to a Brussels sprout?" turns into the Instagram caption, "that feeling when you just want to eat again because you had a terrible dinner" accompanied by a picture of the two of you at a fast-food drive-through.

This is maybe the harshest reality of the internet that we all must come to terms with. The internet is not mean. The comment section of the newspaper is not mean. Those are people. Actual people. People who were in our society before the internet. People are doing mean things in those places, and that meanness builds on itself. Sometimes, those people are us.

Would we have complained the same way about that athlete if no one could hear us? Do we exaggerate our feelings of disgust with a dinner that was served to us so that we can get more likes? What does that do to the person who served it?

Don't just take my word for it. As this book is being written, YouTube has removed the "dislike" button from its videos because their research has shown that people dislike videos at a far lower rate when they can't tell how many people have disliked it already. Judging people negatively is, apparently, contagious.

We don't have a common sense for this. We don't have established social rules about how we govern the meaner instincts that we all have. We don't, many of us, have established social mores that tell us we shouldn't post or comment.

I'm not suggesting that people need to start thinking about each other in kinder, more prosocial ways. That'd be great if that happened, but what I'm suggesting is we need to understand how our values are attached to the new reach we have with our casual commentary. Knowing how we're contributing and how our negativity affects the wider tone of the internet would be a great start.

On the internet, we are always walking by the lockers where people are talking about someone else. Not all of us assume the snickering is about us, but enough of us do that it means your negativity will affect someone. I'm not saying that has to bother you. I'm saying that if it does bother you, you shouldn't do it. If you value goodwill or if you think people's happiness is important, then you need to understand how your online actions affect that.

An offhand remark can have far deeper repercussions in a digital world. Justine Sacco's story is as good as any to serve as a warning for not being careful with what you post. Before boarding a plane to South Africa in 2013, she tweeted, "Going to Africa. Hope I don't get AIDS. Just kidding. I'm white!"

She claims that she was making fun of the insularity of Americans and that people had racist beliefs about diseases in Africa. No matter. By the time she landed, there were tens of thousands of comments and retweets. #HasJustineLandedYet was trending, and she was fired from her job as a communications director. No one asked her to clarify. She didn't get a chance to rephrase it or even give it an ironic tone. The internet mob attacked, and her life was changed forever.

This is an entirely new problem.

We are always learning through our interactions with each other. Some of that learning is formal in-the-classroom learning. Most of it, however, is just a by-product of interaction. I see how you do this. I watch you do that. Our community is always our curriculum, whatever that community happens to be. Every time we are casually mean, our community gets a bit meaner; every time we patiently try and explain that science is a real thing in response to someone, our community sees a bit more of that.

In a connected, digital world, we are always someone who someone else is learning from.

Our learning pool used to be much more restricted by the people who directly and physically surrounded us. Now, that community lives everywhere. And we are constantly being what other people are learning, with every keystroke into the machine.

And those are the things that you do on the internet that you are doing on purpose.

Your conscious posts make up a small part of the information that you are creating. You could, if you had more self-control than I do, make it so that you don't ever post anything that could negatively affect anyone else. But, even if you only ever watch the internet and never post, you are still sending out reams of data that are being collected by hordes of different people. You are becoming a digital identity, all the time.

Some of those folks collecting data are, I believe, honestly trying to use that data to make your online experience better than it was before. That used to be my job. I was responsible for a university website. We would track every search that was done on our website and see where that search led. If it went somewhere unhelpful, we tweaked the search engine to try and improve it. Were we a little biased? Sure. But 87 percent of what we were doing was trying to help.

For some people, your data is a kind of currency. They collect your data as an exchange for the use of the product they are offering you. You may not know that's the deal that you've struck, but you probably signed away your rights at some point when choosing their product. Terms of service? Click yes, and then they can use that data.

Most email services, many social media services, and even some services that you may have paid for make you pay for your service with your data. There are some that take your data for their own purposes that, frankly, have nothing to do with you. Others collect or steal your data with the intent to do something directly to you. And, of course, these categories are not mutually exclusive.

There are some excellent resources available if you are interested in digging deeper into this question, but there's one issue that might help frame things a little. You are not only giving your data to the website you are currently on. You are potentially giving your data to a completely different company that buys the data from the people you have given it to, or you are losing your data to a hacker who steals it. The internet is the world's biggest bathroom wall. Anything on it will be seen by someone at some point.

Let's create an educational website to use as an example. We'll call it Mathstronaut.

The founders of Mathstronaut have decided that after twenty years of experience with university-age science students, they believe that a deep understanding of algebra is the secret to getting good grades in the sciences. When you sign up on the website, there is a tracker downloaded to your desktop that keeps track of everything you do while using the site and gives you a detailed report about your working habits. That tracker also has a record of everything you do in your browser when you are logged into their website (this is pretty common practice).

As you use the site and have a great time doing algebra, the tracker not only notices which questions you get wrong or right, but it also keeps track of how long you take with each question and which questions lead you to search for new knitting patterns before answering. It tracks your Google searches in case you are looking to search engines for answers to the questions. In effect, it replicates some of the actions that would be taken by an interested instructor who was watching you every second that you were working. It uses all this information to power its AI to create challenges for and presents you with access to the information you need to get algebra figured out.

It is "personalizing" your learning.

At the end of the month, the tracker produces a report that tells you what parts of algebra you should focus on (based on the questions that caused you to get distracted or slowed you down). It also gives you a report of how many times you searched for an answer or played Wordle. You had no idea that you were so distractible. This website is having a profound impact on your work and is making you a better student. Yay!

This is a typical sales pitch for a math website. For the purposes of our pretend website, we're going to assume that it actually does the things it claims. Please note: this does not exist. There are ways in which some software does parts of the things described here, but it's mostly generalizations and guesswork. I'm using a "perfect" example to give the website the best possible chance in our scenario.

Now, let's look at how that website is made. The long and legalese "terms of service" that you signed when you created your account gave the creators of the website the right to use your data. As educational researchers, they are intending to use your data to help the whole world with algebra. This means you could send your child or your students to do some work on the website, and everything that they do belongs to the group of people who have made the website. Who cares right? It's not like teachers keep the worksheets that students do in their classrooms. (Don't tell anyone we throw out all the work students do—it's bad for morale.)

The "not-internet" equivalent to this sounds a little weird, but it bears considering. Imagine a group of strangers knocks on the door to your home. They give you a pile of worksheets and say, "Look, give these worksheets to your kid. We'll wait here in the back of your living room and watch. When they're done, we'll take the worksheets into the hallway and correct them and come back in with another worksheet that will provide additional questions based on the answers that they gave us the first time. While we're waiting, we're just going to take notes about what you have here in your living room. We're just going to go ahead and keep a copy of all this information for our files. No rush. We can do this all day."

You might wonder why exactly these people are taking their time to give you this much help. You might want to ask them why they felt the need to keep a copy of everything that was going on in your living room.

And yet.

We have all become accustomed to trading our data for free services on the internet. We give our browser data to Facebook so we can check in on our friends and frenemies. Facebook uses that data to advertise the things we checked out online in our last Google search. Some people even claim that our phones can listen in on us and then tell Facebook what to market back to us. It's called remarketing. It's weird, and a little unsettling, but it isn't enough for most people to lose connections to other people. I do it. I probably shouldn't, given what I do for a living, but I like checking in on my old friends from my teaching days in South Korea.

But when you think about it, what are these people doing this work for? Sure, they are going to do "research," but research for whom? What is the goal of this research? Can you have any confidence that this research is going to be used for the good of the education system? Are they looking for new ways to make kids learn better? Are they trying to find out how to make students use the website more? More math is better, right? But is it? Even if it helps the students do better on tests, does it make up for the trade-off of having those people standing in our living rooms watching our kids?

The reasons why people are providing us with these "free" services are important. If they are making money based on how many ads we click or how much data we post, that is going to change the way they develop the website.

It is super easy to give away our data. We have so much of it, why not give it away so that we can have fun math websites or so we can have a way to check in on how cute (or not cute) the new baby is?

Maybe they are taking that data for a good reason. Maybe they are working on a paper that will change the face of math education. There's a problem though. One of two things tends to be true: either a company is making money from their website and their intent is to keep you using the website, regardless of whether learning is taking place, or they are doing a research project that is going to end at some point.

If they have a profit motive, success for that company is not your learning. Success is profit. They might make money by charging you to use their service. They might make money by selling the lessons they've developed based on your students' use patterns and data. They might be selling the whole company to the highest bidder and including the students' data in the deal.

If, on the other hand, this is a research project, the website is probably going to go away the moment the research is done. That research group will move on to other work. Few things have halted the progress of good educational technology practice more than researchers who have started a research project to "test a theory" that didn't work out the way they hoped. I am guilty as charged on this one. But even worse, some resources go away not because they don't work but because there's no longer funding available once the research is complete.

One way or the other, a picture of your child, or you, has been created in the data. That data can be combined with other data pictures. These sets of data give marketers a subtle sense of who you are. And this is true of vast swaths of our population. There are pictures of most of us out there that provide information about what we like, what we don't like, and what our tendencies are. And we've given it to them. Every personality test and every answered quiz can be combined with other traces of our identity, forming a detailed map of our behavior.

And then the real magic happens.

Armed with an agenda, a subtle understanding of the tendencies of millions of people, and a little disinformation, we can work wonders. The real power of the new abundance starts to shine.

If we can use the data we've collected from you to send you the perfect message, whether it be a lie or a stretch of the truth, that gives us a *much* better chance of selling you something. Whether that something is a cupcake or a political view.

We've been doing this for a long time. Hawkers on the side of the street have been noticing your interest in a particular carpet for hundreds of years. We have legislation in place that specifically stops companies from targeting children with their cigarette alternatives. It is in the interest of every person who is selling something to get in front of people who might buy that thing they are selling. The tools you might have developed for dealing with TV advertising and the street hawker are different. The ways of dealing with web targeting are different again.

Let's say we're in the business of selling cupcakes. You and I have just figured out the secrets behind packing and shipping the perfect cupcake, and we want to get wildly rich in the process.

We've spent years figuring out how to get the cupcake into the mail without the frosting rubbing off on the box. We've stolen the perfect icing recipe from season seven of the Great British Bake Off, and we have the cake recipe that my grandma used to make. We're set. Right? We buy bulletproofcupcakes.com, and we're good to go. Cupcakes. Come and get 'em.

But no one comes. My mom orders a cupcake. We convince a few of our friends to try the cupcakes just to make sure the website is actually working, but that's it.

Advertising. That's what we need.

After looking at the two interfaces for the most effective web advertising (Google and Facebook), we decide to try Facebook. We get ourselves an account and pay ten bucks a day for Facebook to deliver ads to people about our cupcakes.

So, what have we done?

Well, in setting up our ad, we might have chosen to break down our target market a little: people under the age of forty-five are most likely to buy cupcakes on the internet. (I have no idea if this is true, but you probably don't know either.) We told Facebook to go out and find people who search for desserts during their workday and who completed a quiz called "What kind of cupcake are you?"

There are about a billion people who have Facebook accounts. Each of them has registered for "free" software that allows them to check in on their high school crush, see people's babies, and hate-like people's travel photos in exchange for their data. In exchange for all of this, each person gives them access to their eyes. Each person on Facebook has agreed to this whether they know they have or not.

And we at bulletproofcupcakes.com have now bought access to their eyes. That's great, right? Who doesn't like cupcakes?

As long as we're talking about cupcakes, maybe it is great. But what if the topic was voting and someone was looking to influence the views of a million people on a particular subject? Or what if someone decided that discouraging people from getting vaccinated was better for their own product? What if there was a massive referendum in your country to see if you were going to stay in Europe (to use a random, maybe not made-up example), and you were interested in trying to make people vote to leave that continent (search "Cambridge Analytica" for this story)? What if you created a personality profile quiz for Facebook and used that information to target different types of people in ways that they were particularly susceptible?

The argument goes like this: if we are all confronted by hundreds (thousands) of things that we need to decide quickly, we don't have much time to commit to making those decisions. People are targeting us with disinformation regarding those decisions for reasons of profit or political orientation. They are targeting us based on the data that we are sending out with every click of our keyboard. This has a complex and detrimental effect on our society.

We get overloaded. They take advantage of it.

One way or the other, we need to understand it. The abundance of information has changed the way that people seek to influence us, and we need to be able to deal with it. When we put our data together with the disinformation that people are trying to send us, bad things are going to happen.

We still need to be able to learn. But we have to learn differently.

CHAPTER 4

This Is at Least Partially an Education Problem

In 2007, an article was published in the *Harvard Business Review* suggesting that deliberate practice, 10,000 hours over the course of fifteen to twenty-five years, creates "expertise." To accomplish this, you need the opportunity, some luck, and a fair amount of privilege. But taken broadly, if you do something lots and lots, you become good at it. It's a theory that was popularized by Malcolm Gladwell and was all the rage a few years ago. Like many "theories of how we learn," the original research makes cautious claims but gets overblown when it hits the media.

I'm going to make an even more limited claim: if you do something for 10,000 hours, you get used to it.

It just so happens that there is a public institution that forces people (by law in many countries) to go and do something for 10,000 hours. A common school year lasts between 175 and 190 days. If you count approximately 5 hours of actual instruction a day over 12 years, you get well over 10,000 hours. Think about that: well over 10,000 hours of doing the same thing in a structured way. You must be learning something. You could be an expert at it if you were deliberate about it.

School!

For whatever math or social studies you might remember from those years, you also have a sense of what school *is*. Your idea of what it means to learn is shaped by your own experience in our education systems. You've learned both math and "the game" of school.

You've learned that tests are what we give students to see if they've learned. You've learned that teachers tell you what they want you to remember and then check to see if you remembered. You've learned, as a student of mine once said, that no adult ever asks a child a question without already knowing the answer. Teachers are knowers. Students are learners. You've learned all kinds of sitting and hand-raising behaviors. You've learned that doing what you're told is what gets you good grades.

Most of all, you've learned that someone already knows what you need to know, *and* they can tell you if you got it right.

Learning, as I'm using the word here, is something that happens as a side effect of being a human. There are tons of different definitions of it, and lots of clever scientists spend piles of other people's money trying to figure out exactly how it works inside of our brains. Let's keep the definition open for now. You keep yours, and I'll keep mine, and we'll talk a little more about learning together.

I know that probably hurts. I've been in many debates over the years where people say things like, "How can we possibly talk about this without first deciding on a definition?" Here's the thing: We aren't going to agree. You and I might, but generally, we're not going to. You could say, "Hey, this is what it says in the dictionary!" I could respond, "Yeah, but that doesn't include this other thing." Two hours from now, our conversation has gotten nowhere.

It's hard. That's a lot of uncertainty to have at the middle of an institution as important as education.

We've lost the moment in time (if we ever had it) where we could have one definition of a concept like learning. I could get a definition of learning from a university professor, but I might be leaving out the ideas of the Indigenous elder I worked with last fall. It doesn't mean the word doesn't "mean" anything; it means that it means many things at the same time. It also means that we can sometimes agree on what we think learning isn't.

I see education as something different than learning. For me, education is the process by which we, as a society, create the norms we think are important. Norms of information. Norms of knowledge. Norms of behavior. You could say it's a system for "learning," but that would mean at some level that there is someone who thought about what learning is and created a system for it. As if learning was a monolith that we could build a system for. As if there was a single person or group responsible for that system. As if learning was like money and could be counted.

Maybe education is built as an environment for what some people call learning, but I have a sneaking suspicion that this is only because we've all spent so much time in that system. We now believe it's for learning because it's the system we have.

What we actually have is a long line of people, some well-meaning and some not so much, who are interested in the idea of public education. Many of them have norms they think are important, that they think everyone else should have. Our schools are an extension of who we are as a culture, but they are also an amalgam of all the things that we have been. Some of those are great things, some are decisions that were made as a matter of convenience, and some are things that we should leave far behind. And, to be fair, there are lots of great educators in the system right now who are trying to adjust the system we have to respond to the needs that our students have today.

The education system is, fundamentally, a bureaucratic challenge. With millions of students to organize, thousands of teachers to support, and the entirety of the human experience to choose from in terms of what to teach, it's a daunting task. It would be nice if there was a pile of research that we could use to guide us in this, and there is, from a certain point of view. But that research is often contradictory, and it depends heavily on your own perspective of what you think learning is. Because of this, we tend to rely on what we've done in the past. We tweak. We iterate. We refine. We regress.

Often, those tweaks and iterations don't last very long because 10,000 hours of being trained in something is a strong pull. You will not come across a pile of schools (proportionally) that are truly setting out on a new model for education. Parents often don't want school to be radically different from the experience they had as students. Kids who understand the game of school don't want people moving the markers of success. Teachers don't have time for change, especially when the latest revolution is launched half-baked into the schools without any context or connection to last year's revolution.

Several challenges limit the possibility for change. You have curriculum developers who are trying to meet the needs of as many kinds of people as possible. You have different ideas of what learning is inside the system. You have a large portion of the population who thinks that students should be taught *the exact same thing* they were taught in school. Ask a parent about "new math" and see what happens. Just, you know, find a comfortable chair before you do.

In over twenty years of teaching, administrating, and consulting, I've met very few people inside the education system who don't care about students. It's just that everyone has a different idea about what caring should look like.

I'm not going to try and convince you that the education system is or isn't one thing or another. I'm suggesting that the system has fundamentally shaped how we view learning. As we explore how our system has been shaped, we'll see that most of the shaping has been designed to solve the problem of information scarcity. Our experience of learning in "education" has not prepared us for dealing with abundance. Our education system teaches us that things are true. And that someone else can tell you when you got something right.

Learning is not something that is done to someone. It's not "education."

Learning is, maybe, an extension of what it is to be human. It allows us to adapt to our environments, become better people, and understand how to play a new video game. Learning is not always a good thing. We can learn that stealing is something we can get away with. We can learn that lying can get you elected. We can learn how to lie more effectively. We can learn that the world is a cold, dark place. We can learn things that are simply not true.

That last piece is important. Learning and adaptability have no necessary connection to what is good for us. Much like reading, learning can be good. It's probably good more often than it is bad. But learning and reading on their own are not implicitly good. Lots of terrible things have been done, at least partially, based on what someone has learned or read.

At its broadest, an "education" is getting the experiences and information you need to be a member of your society. In ancient Rome, it was customary for a young man (and it was always men) to accompany his father to the Roman Forum to get a sense of how a young man was supposed to act. The young men would watch how their fathers interacted with colleagues, employees, followers, and people they followed. This was the education that they needed to sustain their place in the status quo. As they got older, an older man, often a family friend or associate, would act as a mentor and help them with their early steps into adulthood. According to the little we know of Caesar's biography, it seems that discipline and respect, other parts of their education, were taught by their mother. What did Caesar learn? Well, he learned that if you have power, you can do whatever you want. He learned it to the extent that he took down the whole Roman Republic with him. Probably not what his relatives intended for him to learn nor what they thought they were teaching.

Every version of an education system has values baked into it. It's also, often, an interesting insight into the constraints of a particular society. In the eduba (scribal school) of ancient Mesopotamia, the goal was standardization. Those schools were mostly about teaching cuneiform, which is, give or take, the first symbol-based writing system in history. If you're creating what amounts to the first (or firstish) writing system, you've got to want everyone to agree what a symbol means. If we all use a different symbol for fish, for example, then the writing system is not much good. There are thousands of extant clay tablets from these schools that show learners practicing these words over and over. Practice making lines. Practice making syllables. At the advanced level, we see a different view of what was valued in those schools. Advanced students at an eduba in Nippur (1740 BCE) memorized the Decad, ten famous stories from Sumerian literature. This would, presumably, mean that your scribe could be depended upon to know these stories to tell, or perhaps rewrite, from memory.

These two goals, standardization and memorization, make total sense in a society where writing is just starting to become something people understand.

When Europe started peeking its way through the veil of the Dark Ages, one of the first things heard about learning came from the court of Charlemagne (circa 789 CE). Many priests in his day couldn't speak biblical Latin. While the Franks (French) used to speak Latin as a mother tongue, what they were speaking by this time was starting to sound suspiciously like Old French. This did not stop priests from saying Latin phrases when performing important ceremonies. Those phrases did things like make marriages official and make sure babies didn't go to hell—so they were important phrases. The priests recited them as best as they could remember them, but they were not doing a great job. Charlemagne, a very religious sort, thought God could only speak biblical Latin and figured that if the priests said the phrases wrong, those phrases wouldn't work.

Stopping babies from going to hell is important work.

In his attempt to reform the learning level of the clergy, Charlemagne released the "Charter of Modern Thought" in 789 CE. It led to all kinds of things, including better education for bishops, enforced education for priests, and eventually, schools to be opened at monasteries for kids. It also led to standardized tests for priests to make sure they understood the basics of what they were supposed to be doing.

We don't know exactly what happened at those schools, so it's difficult to make a direct connection between them and our current education system. There is one slightly terrifying story of one pupil who burned down the monastery to avoid being disciplined for a now forgotten crime. In almost every case we know of, however, students in the monastery schools were learning things about God or other people whom the church respected (like Boethius and St. Augustine). They also learned chanting. And how to calculate what day Easter falls on. These are all things that were seen as important in their time. At this point, the clever reader probably sees where this is going.

In the twelfth and thirteenth centuries, we saw the vague beginnings of the modern university. At almost the same time, we saw the birth of thought control at universities. There is one school of historical thought that sees the founding of universities as directly tied to the desire for thought control. In their version, the church and local rulers encouraged the formal formation of universities to avoid the tedious problem of having to track down local smart people teaching the masses and causing trouble (search for Peter Abelard—one of history's greatest, and least self-reflective, troublemakers). While those "universities" did not start out as big fancy buildings where everyone attended classes, the teachers' affiliation with the university made it so that they could be surveilled by the church, and the content could be better controlled. Aristotle's *Physics* was banned at the University of Paris, for instance, because it taught an origin story that conflicted with church teachings.

The church wanted to control what people were learning.

We take up our incredibly brief history of education in 1798 with my favorite educator, Johann Heinrich Pestalozzi. He had a dream . . . and what a dream. He wanted to teach the entirety of Switzerland to read (and 'rite and do 'rithmatic—the three Rs). Pestalozzi had a tricky problem, though: he didn't have many teachers to work with. In his book *How Gertrude Teaches Her Children*, he talks about his solution. Imagine, Pestalozzi considers, if we took all the things that people needed to know and broke them into small pieces—pieces defined so simply that anyone, whether they understood what they were doing or not, could teach someone else how to do something by following along with the book. Let's just go ahead and call it a "textbook." (I added that textbook part. To my knowledge he never said that.)

In each of those circumstances, we open a window into a culture when we look at its education system. The Mesopotamians needed standardization. Charlemagne tried to fix his country's relationship with God. The church tried to use the university to control how its doctrines were being taught. And our friend Pestalozzi tried to help his country read—he just needed to bake the approach to teaching into his content because he had so few teachers to work with.

Each of these stories, of course, only looks at part of what is happening in any society or culture. I'm sure there were different ways of teaching on a farm in 789 CE, but no record of this survives. People also learned things from their parents and the neighbors they apprenticed with. We are always only looking at parts of the story.

It would be impossible (foolish, and even arrogant) to try and talk about what our education system is in the year 2024. What I do think brings all of those examples together, however, is that in each of those cases, they were trying to teach everyone in those learning environments the same thing. I want you to remember these ancient tales. Do your best to remember them exactly. In controlling how you were seeing a religious interpretation, I want you to remember this particular interpretation.

Think of all the ways we relate "learning" with "remembering" in our world. We worry when doctors check their phones for information because they haven't remembered what to do. We give kids tests to see if they can remember what we told them in a classroom two months ago. We see people who remember facts on a quiz show as smart. Our teaching structures have almost always been about how to give people the things they need so they can store them in their memories. It's a transaction, whether as a kind act of giving or a cynical act of pushing one particular view of the world.

And sure, remembering things is useful. There are educational experts out there right now who will tell you that remembering is *super important* for our education system (e.g., Daniel Willingham). Remembering is a great way to keep information with you. It is a great way of dealing with the problem of information scarcity. But is it as important as it was when we didn't have an amazing machine in our pocket that has everyone else's memory in it?

We should all remember what has come before us. Our knowledge builds that way. Our history is important. I'm good with all of that. And, truth be told, remembering what has been done before has a long tradition in universities. Let's take up the early university thread that we dropped earlier.

Scholasticism was the dominant view of learning at the dawn of the university in Europe in the twelfth and thirteenth centuries. The Scholastics believed that all things written in the canonical religious texts (e.g., the Bible, books by the Fathers of the Church) were true. If a point of confusion or conflict between two different pieces of scripture was raised, it was the responsibility of the students to explain away the confusion. In the Scholastic view, the books could not be wrong. The flaw was in the reasoning. The work of the intellectual, of the good thinker, of the responsible knower, was to remember everything in those books and explain why these old books are right.

This is a "looking back" way of deciding if things are true. It's an appeal to collective knowledge and existing wisdom. There's certainly a lot of value in this approach, but it does limit us to the view of the world that we had before. It also supposes that someone somewhere knows what the "truth" is.

Think of the way that fans of current cultural phenomena like Marvel or Star Wars consider their movies. They consider things from books and movies as "canon," meaning they are true. Other things are considered as "retcon" (retroactive continuity), meaning that something has taken a different interpretation of a "canon" event to open a new part of the story. These things can be the start of many long, tedious arguments as fans scramble to both complain about the changed "truth" and then struggle to make them all fit into their new understanding of the world.

Old things good; new things bad.

The job of the student in a Scholastic view is to acquire the accepted knowledge that has already been approved in the canon. Think of the classic academic paper. Make sure that every claim is cited. Don't say anything that doesn't already appear in someone else's work. If it's not part of the canon, it can't be included in the paper.

Balancing against the Scholastics in the history of the university are the humanists. In them, you will see the word *humanities*, which is a word that is, in our era, a little more fashionable than *Scholasticism*. The humanists are more a product of the fourteenth-century upheaval that came after the Black Death.

They questioned some of the foundations of "knowledge" as it was understood in their time. They started to notice that some of the knowledge in old books didn't match their experiences. They could tell, for instance, that the description of the human body they inherited was not correct. They could see it in their dissection rooms. The old maps of the world started to become outdated as European explorers followed the paths of earlier explorers and found new lands outside of the understanding of the Greeks and Romans.

The humanists believed that learners, on their own, could come to understand new things that hadn't been discovered before. Learning was more of an exploration.

There's no reason not to see a happy tension between Scholasticism as respect for what has gone before and humanism as a quest for what we can still know. You could think of a balance between the two as rigor balanced by creativity. You could see it as enthusiasm balanced by respect for those who have gone before you. It's not a bad balance, but the shifts back and forth affect all our discussions about what it means to learn.

In practice, though, the "respect for what has gone before" works a little easier in our education system. I can get you to read all about a particular piece of chemistry and see if you remember what I said. It is much more difficult for me to get you to "explore" science to find something new. You need to know *so much* before you can do that.

When we move from the word *learning* to the word *education*, we run into one of the stickiest parts of this whole story: grades. We think of them as a general marker for how smart someone is or how much a person has learned. Grades are fundamental to understanding the system of education. They are our proof. They are our evidence in the evidence-based learning process.

But if I asked you what your grades were in high school, which of the two concepts of education would I be talking about: Scholasticism or humanism? As the testing usually measures classroom content, we'd mostly be talking about what you remembered. We'd be talking about what parts of the old books you'd managed to prove, at that time, that you could remember.

Creativity is tough to measure. Creativity is also really inconvenient to plan for in a classroom. I can force a classroom full of kids to be quiet and listen to me, but it's another thing entirely to "force" people to take initiative and be creative.

When we think about bureaucratizing the whole system of education, it's easier for us to base it on people remembering things. Creativity is an ephemeral thing that each of us approaches differently, whereas the recall kind of memory is something I can ask you on a test and check to see if you've done it. The answer on a recall test is going to be the same for everyone. I look at your paper, and it's there or it isn't.

As we look out over the challenges we are facing today, whether dealing with our impact on the climate or figuring out how to be polite at the dinner table with our phones, we're going to need some of that creativity and ability to adapt. We can't "remember" how to approach those problems. There may be hundreds of different perspectives on how we should be addressing the issues we are confronting, so we're going to need to be able to "choose" and not just "remember."

But if we're thinking about how we teach and learn now, how do we help people learn to make choices when there aren't obvious answers? How do we choose what to include and what to leave out? How do we talk about things that are uncertain and will always be uncertain? Is it really necessary to keep all that stuff in our heads? Who does this serve?

Thanks for asking.

We started this journey together with me wondering what the content of my course was "supposed" to be in those first classes I taught in South Korea. I didn't know the expert who knew the answer, so I wasn't sure if I was doing it the right way. How was I to decide from a world full of options brought to me through an internet full of web pages? Are there "right" things for me to teach about English? Should I teach Australian English? Should I be preparing their English for a conversation over ice cream or a courtroom?

From a learner's perspective, it's mostly about making the teacher happy. The answer might change depending on whether I want an A+ or a D−, but success is measurable for most. The job of the learner is to figure out what content is important to the teacher and prove that I have retained that content. It's the game of school. Give the teacher what they want. Get the grade.

Does that prepare us for an information scarce society? Uh . . . maybe. It certainly taught me that I would be rewarded for doing what I was told, a lesson, I'm afraid, that has only had a limited impact. It taught me that success in the education system is attained by being compliant and accepting the course content as true. Or, at least, true for the course.

That view of content made sense in the eduba and in the thirteenth-century classroom, but does it help us learn the way we need to learn today? It's certainly how we currently measure it. You get an A for remembering the content and doing what you're told. That's how I know you've learned. I can just look at your grade.

And we need to know if we have learned, right?

Our bosses want to know if we learned things in the course they paid for. Parents need to know that their child is getting good grades. The school board needs measurable data that tells them their students are improving. The government needs to know that teachers are doing their job and schools are "improving." Students need to be able to see that they are learning.

Let's assume that every one of those things is true for education. That the education *system* requires those things. Does the need to measure learning make measuring learning possible?

We have this built-in belief that learning is something we can measure. That it's about getting things "right" and solving the problem. That there is both something out there that is "right" and someone who can tell me if it's right. That's what we have learned from our 10,000 hours in an education system.

1. The right answer exists.
2. There are people who can tell me that I have the right answer.

If this is what we learn "learning" is, we are going to struggle when we hit real-world kinds of problems. You can go ahead and spend years looking for someone who is going to tell you that you are a "good" parent or that you have the right taste in furniture.

We certainly have other models in education. Educators have phrases like "formative feedback" and "positive reinforcement" that speak to different ways to encourage people. They just don't give us that satisfied "Ah . . . I'm done learning" feeling.

Formative assessment is, broadly speaking, the kind of assessment that intends to help a student learn something over time. It is the kind of feedback that you give someone to suggest that they do something a bit differently. For example, you may advise them to do more reading in a particular area with the idea that you're going to check in on them again later. Someone tries something, and you say, "Hey, try this." They try it again, do it in a way you approve of, and you say, "Yup, that's better." It's "formative" in the sense that you are "forming them" to your idea of what "doing it right" looks like.

Let's stick to cooking for our examples. Let's say that I'm watching you cook pasta sauce in my kitchen. Let's also say you're foolish enough to ask my advice about your cooking. You're chopping away, and I stop you and say, "Well, you might want to consider frying those onions first and waiting on the garlic. The onions are going to take longer to cook, and if you put them in at the same time at high heat, you're going to burn the garlic." Now, I might be wrong about that. It's possible that cooks all over the world know that I'm wrong, but that is my perspective. And you asked.

Now, I have just given you a formative assessment. I have "formed" your understanding of making pasta sauce and have helped you produce a pasta sauce that is different from what would have happened otherwise. Hopefully, if I know what I'm talking about, it's better than what you would have otherwise produced. Formative assessment often happens when the task is not yet complete. You still have time to make the sauce better.

Alternately, I could be tasting your first pasta sauce and saying, "Huh, I kinda feel like you put the garlic in a little too early. There's a slightly bitter taste in here that I think comes from burnt garlic." Now, this is a summative assessment. I have "assessed" your sauce after it is finished. You may feel that burnt garlic is what makes a pasta sauce. That's your opinion, not mine. I'm in charge. Those are decisions that I make.

A summative assessment is what happens when you are finished with a particular task. I have tasted your pasta sauce, and it's bad. It tastes like burnt garlic. Way to ruin dinner.

In a formative assessment model, I am sharing what I think I know with you in an attempt to make you a better pasta sauce maker. It's not exactly critical that I'm right about it (you could, for instance, fry those onions and garlic on low heat, and they won't burn). It's structured mentoring. I'm passing along what I know to you so that you can get better at the thing that you are doing.

In a summative assessment model, I have decided what is "right," and I am going to decide if what you are doing matches up with what I think is right. If we think back to our Scholastics, we'll remember that they thought they had the information they needed, and they knew they had access to "right things." To be a summative assessor, you need to know the correct answer.

So, back to learning. In a formative model, learning is something that happens in social interaction (however structured), and you, hopefully, get better pasta sauce. In a summative model, learning is the accrual of the knowledge that the instructor has either in their head or has been given by someone else. There is one universal pasta sauce that you are trying to make. Or, to be fair, there are many universal pasta sauces, and you need to cite which one it was you were trying to make . . . as long as you make it the way that your assessor believes you should make it.

Testing is a weird thing when you think about it. We sometimes see the results of a test as a direct reflection of what someone "knows." Does that mean that someone is prepared for life in some way that someone else isn't? Is there a straight line between a person's ability to perform on a test and their ability to be happy? Well, maybe. But it's certainly not necessary.

Think about it. Most assignments or tests you have ever done work like this:

1. The teacher gives you a question to which they have already decided what the right answer is.
2. They hide the answer from you.
3. They tell you not to talk to anyone else about your answer.
4. They see if you give them the exact answer they want.
5. They reward you based on how well you conformed to what they wanted.

When I say it that way, does it sound prosocial? Does that sound like how you want things to work in your house or at your job? More importantly, even if it was the greatest idea in the world, it can't really work anymore.

I mean, historically, grades weren't really about learning at all. They were about encouraging students to do the work. It's an extrinsic motivator (one that motivates you from the outside). It is the way that we as arbiters of the education system motivate students about what they should learn, when they should learn, and, inevitably, what it means to have learned. I got an A. I learned.

The opposite of an extrinsic motivator is an intrinsic motivator. If I'm intrinsically motivated, then I'm motivated to do the learning for myself. Phil Schlechty, the director of an American educational research institute, has a model I find useful for talking about this. In his model, he makes the distinction between five levels of learner engagement. While the model was designed for the classroom, I've found it useful as a way of thinking about any kind of learning.

1. Intrinsic motivation: I'm doing this for my own purposes.
2. Strategic compliance: I'm going to understand the game of school to get the grades I want.
3. Ritual compliance: I'll learn what I have to so I don't get in trouble.
4. Retreatism: I'm not really engaged.
5. Rebellion: I'm purposefully trying to mess this up for everyone else.

I find our view of the education system is often trapped at number two in this process. If we do assignments or tests that have predetermined right answers that the teacher is hiding, we fall into the category of strategic compliance. In that view, success is coming up with what someone else has told you to believe. Someone else knows the answer, and your job is to give them the answer that they want.

Grading is good at encouraging people to do complicated tasks that are often represented by memorization, obedience, and linear thinking. If those are our actual goals, then that approach is likely to be the most successful. If our goals are complex and include things like creativity, we're looking to support intrinsic motivation. Summative grading makes people want to do what they're told. It makes them want to work Scholastically.

While working on a creativity project this summer, I was talking to an excellent educator who said, "Look, I know you don't want to put grades on this, but if you don't, the teachers won't teach it." If you can't grade it, it can't be taught. If it's not taught, well, you see where this is going.

Creativity is not a counting noun. Did you get seven or eight creativities today at school, Helen? People do try and measure it. Our system demands it. The system doesn't care if we can't measure a thing. It wants us to measure it anyway. Common custom is to create a list of things for a student to do called a rubric and then check the student's actions against it. "Dave showed a moderate amount of originality in his book, six out of ten." But that number is still a number I just made up against a system for measurement that I made up. And those made-up numbers have a profound effect on what we learn and what we can learn. It's much easier for me as a teacher to use a multiple choice test than to make up an imaginary measurement system for how engaged a student is or how much they care about their work.

People will tell you that there are "evidence-based" approaches to assessment. It sounds good, doesn't it? I want to have some nice concrete evidence before I go and learn something so I can make the best use of my time. That's what you'd want people to do. Imagine if the police didn't use evidence to arrest people or if lawyers didn't use evidence to defend people. Evidence is easier to apply to some things than others.

If Jane is arrested for stealing a hundred bucks from your wallet, there would be evidence. At its simplest level, maybe there's a recording of her opening your car door, grabbing your wallet, and pulling out your money. This is nice concrete evidence. Let's say that we don't have anything so perfect as a recording, but we know that Jane was in the parking lot. We know that she needs money to pay off a debt, and she suddenly has a hundred bucks that she didn't have before. All that evidence is "circumstantial" evidence. The fact that those things are true doesn't mean she took the money from you. It's not clear proof. But here's the thing: either Jane stole the money, or she didn't. There is a fact in the world. We may not know if Jane stole the money, but she does. She did. Or she didn't. Jane, at least, knows the truth.

The evidence that we want for evidence-based learning must be built on the same foundation. There must be a "thing" that we have evidence of. If, for example, we are trying to measure student attendance, then I don't have a problem. Either the kid went to school or they didn't. If you made a change (let's say you start school fifteen minutes later) and student absences in the first class of the day decrease by 20 percent, you've got yourself an excellent evidence-based piece of change right there. If you're measuring student happiness with a survey, an increase in student-reported happiness may or may not reflect "real" happiness. However, your addition of cookies and quiet rooms may impact reported happiness. And that's a real thing. You can see that a kid reported their happiness.

But what if the thing you are looking to measure is complex? Like learning. Let's set the bar for this exploration as low as we possibly can. Let's say that we think "learning" is the ability to remember a thing that the teacher said and repeat it in response to a multiple-choice question on a test. There are certainly people who see education in this way. If we all think back to our own educational experiences, this was often the bar for what we considered learning to be.

Let's say that the adaptation we're going to make is that we are going to have the teacher repeat each item to be remembered at least five times during any class. It's the trendy new "Repeater's Method" of teaching (not a real thing, I hope), and it turns out, schools that have used the Repeater's Method have seen their test scores improve by 7 percent. That's some evidence right there. We have concrete evidence that the Repeater's Method helps people repeat things they heard from a teacher in a classroom. It stands to reason. It's even in the name. The Repeater's Method. Case closed. Let's repeat everything in our classroom at least five times all the time.

That's evidence-based decision making. The Repeater's Method is perfect. It's easy to train people. (Hey, would you just repeat the things on the test over and over again in your class? Good? Thanks.) There are no new schoolbooks that need to be purchased.

Now, I just invented that research approach, and it certainly oversimplifies the research process, but it is not an exaggeration in terms of what a good evidence-based research project is trying to do. This kind of measurement project seeks to pare down all the variables in a research piece as much as possible: get rid of all the other issues clouding the relationship between cause and effect, have a clear measurement, and have something that is repeatable. It is evidence-based *as far as it goes*.

What, though, does it say about learning? Students not only learn to recall (for a short time) the content that you've repeated to them, but they also learn that this *is* learning. Learning is finding out what they are supposed to repeat and then repeating it. They learn that compliance will be rewarded.

They learn that someone else has the answer to a question. Our desire for evidence leads us in this direction. The quantitative research process demands that we remove complexity from the process of research so that we can report on the efficacy of the one thing that we are interested in.

I understand why a person might think that they need evidence for learning. The desire for evidence, however, does not make it possible to get that evidence. Are there certain kinds of learning that can be served by this approach? Sure. But do we want our learning limited by things that we can measure and that we can decide by giving a yes or no answer? I don't think so. It is not the kind of learning that will help us confront uncertainty.

That is not the learning that we need to do on a daily basis. No one is here in our daily lives to tell us what to learn. No one is here to tell us that we got the right answer. Most of the time, we won't even know what the right question is. And, most disturbingly, the right answer to most of our questions doesn't exist.

And I'm not just talking about giant questions regarding climate change or the rise of fascists. I'm referring to everyday problems. How do we decide how to be good friends but still preserve our privacy? How do we keep our hearts open when we can see all the terrible things that are happening in the world? How do we choose to live in a world that has changed around us?

When we feel like we can't get the right answer to our complex questions, a couple of things start to happen:

1. We look for someone else who might have the right answer, and we believe them.
2. We give up on the problem because we can't solve it.

In the first case, we factionalize. We have picked our people who have the right answer and stop thinking through the things that they tell us. The things they say are true because they've said them. Just look around at our political landscape. There's a reason why a "reasoned" argument is often so difficult to find. That's simply not how some people are picking their truths. They are picking someone to believe. You can't argue against belief.

In the second case, we give up. We become apathetic. We decide that because we can't fix the climate, we'll stop trying to do the little things that help. There's no solution, so why bother?

If we change how we look at uncertainty, however, we have a fighting chance to be both reasonable with the things that we believe and hopeful that the things we choose to do can have a positive impact.

We learn to stop trying to "solve" for uncertainty. Instead, we learn to deal with uncertainty.

CHAPTER 5

Societal Implications

In her 2012 book *Alone Together*, author Sherry Turkle worries that we are growing apart from each other and no longer having the deep, meaningful conversations we once had. She sees people on their phones in a coffee shop and thinks they aren't talking to each other.

It's a concern that many of us have at some level. Our social spaces look different than they did before the ubiquitous cell phone came into our lives. You can sit at a counter in a coffee shop or pub and see a line of people staring at their phones. Since the pandemic, the idea of being within six feet of each other and making eye contact has become even more difficult.

I heard a story from a colleague (over Zoom) just before the pandemic about traveling with high school kids. He said things have changed so much in his last ten years of bus trips. There was a time when he used to bring movies on the bus, and the most fun they had was deciding what movie everyone was going to watch. They all watched the movie together, every eye on the screen. Since each person now has a phone in their pocket, the kids shrug their shoulders when the movies come out, and they mostly just stay on their phones. Something was lost. A shared experience has splintered.

I think I agree with Turkle that we aren't always as focused on the people in front of us when we are together. That quiet boredom of a long trip or the in-between spaces of a conversation are mostly things of the past. When given a five-second pause while someone gets up to grab a drink or answer the door, phones come out, and "things are checked." Anxiety is eased. We make sure we haven't missed out.

In the past, those students on the bus were building the shared experience of having watched that movie together, but the ability to curate people's boredom in this way has gotten harder. While on their phones, some students are playing mindless games. Others are creating art. Some are connecting with people, maybe on the same bus using the kind of privacy that is otherwise impossible in a crowded space. I could imagine texting that I'm uncomfortable driving in the dark to my best friend but maybe not saying it out loud.

It's a change, certainly, but is it a net loss?

I think the loss of boredom is definitely a loss. Creating space for boredom is important in everyone's life if you can find something productive to do with it. It can lead to creativity, but it can also lead to destructive behaviors. I'm not sure I want *all* the boredom back.

Those kids on their phones could be talking to someone. And those conversations could be deep, connected conversations. They are just happening in texts. Alternately, we could be having the same superficial conversations on the phone that people are having face-to-face. While I do remember a couple of good conversations on bus trips as a child, the fact that I remember each one tells you how many good ones I had.

I don't think our technology-fueled connections are necessarily worse than the connections we had before. They certainly allowed us to stay connected when the planes stopped flying during COVID.

But they are different. We have new ways of making friends and tracking those friendships. New social norms are emerging.

Text before you call.

You are required to "like" your friends' posts.

Don't leave people "on read."

I am not suggesting that phone-based connections replace face-to-face friendships. I'm saying, like with everything in this book, digital connections exist, and we haven't all learned good common sense about them yet. And, in this world of abundance, a single set of commonsense actions can't be our goal either. People from different cultures with different abilities and needs are going to have other ways of acting that they want us to understand. We don't have that easy reference for the difference between what we can do and what we should do that we may have had forty years ago. We're going to need to learn approaches to learning to work together that we can apply to different people and situations. Approaches that express our values.

There are also new responsibilities. I used to teach digital leadership to residence assistants. One of the conversations we had was about how careful you needed to be as a leader organizing an event in public (meaning on the web). If you go on Facebook and publicly invite three friends to a party, you are automatically leaving out your other friends who can read your post. The same applies to pictures from the event after the fact. If you're having drinks at the pub on a Friday night with a few friends, all of your other friends know they were excluded when they see the photos on Insta.

It's equivalent to walking into a room of ten people and inviting the three people in the middle of the room to come hang out. Though, it's worse than that. At least in the face-to-face case, you know who you excluded. Online, there could be a hundred other people who saw your post and realized they weren't invited. Many of our interactions have become more overtly political because they are public interactions.

In the past, the scarcity of our connections created all kinds of barriers that we have relied on for years. We used to be able to go home from our jobs in ways we just can't today. You can ignore an email from your boss in today's world, but that's a whole new negotiation that you have to make with her. You can pretend to not see a text from your friend because you're not quite ready to answer their question about the weekend getaway, but they are going to start to wonder after thirty minutes or so.

Our new(ish) technologies do offer unprecedented access to other people. Whether those other people have recorded themselves playing video games or they are at the other end of a text message, we can reach someone somewhere at any time. We have an abundance of connections. And that makes our lives different. Different in ways we need to think about.

Abundance creates new uncertainty we need to learn to deal with.

When you really understand something, you understand which rules are unbreakable and which rules are guidelines that apply in a broader sense. We have that expert feeling about our face-to-face encounters but not so much about our digital ones. We know how to apply our values and experience to those face-to-face interactions, but not always to the online ones.

Imagine the face of a child (it could be your face) after a sleepover. They stayed up way later than they let on. They played a bunch of video games, shared some deep secrets about who they "like like," and are altogether overwhelmed and overstimulated. I have no blame for that face or the child behind it. They wanted to make the most of the sleepover they just had. I might smugly tell that child that the reason they feel like garbage is because they didn't go to bed the three times they were told to. But there is something about having access to your friend for long periods of time that allows for a different kind of connection.

That kind of constant, long-term connection is available to any child with a device now. The prolonged contact, the urgent demands for attention, the comfort in knowing you were chosen. They can connect. And connect. And share. They don't have command of the other person's attention in the same way, but they know that person "might" be there the whole time. All of the connection, more uncertainty.

The sleepover from my childhood started and ended. The other child went home. Those are limits put on the connection by time and space. It's not that I didn't want the sleepover to last forever. It just couldn't.

We know the rules of sleepovers. Imagine a child goes to a sleepover and refuses to leave. Imagine that child arrives at 4 p.m., and the receiving parents refuse to feed them. We have tons and tons of norms that we've all mostly accepted. These norms may differ by culture, but norms are accepted within each culture.

Smartphones are a total social game changer for kids.

If we take a Scholastic approach to how we need to help our children handle their phones, if we dig into our history of common sense for an answer, what kind of rules do we come up with? Stop being on your phone at dinner. You can be on the phone for fifteen minutes. Phones out by 10 p.m. Oh, and you can simply take the device away from the teen. I understand that. You can "say" those things, but those rules are difficult to enforce, and they aren't going to address all the issues at hand. They were designed for a different world. A world of connection scarcity.

Look at those choices in the context that the child currently lives in, this current world of connection abundance.

When you went home from that sleepover as a child, you were disconnected. When your child goes home, they are still connected to their friends through their technology. There is no separation. Every unanswered text can feel like being ignored. Any thought you want to share or connection you want to make is seconds away. All the time. Telling someone not to connect is like asking two thirteen-year-olds to sit next to each other and not talk. You can only do it by being aggressive. Or with bribery. Or a great deal of structure.

Because they are, conceptually, sitting in the same room. Every time you tell them not to talk, you're asking them to ignore someone in the room. They are ghosting their friends. The rules of social interaction are not the same as they were twenty years ago. They know they have phone access, text access, and website access to their friends at any moment of the day. From an access perspective, they are in permanent sleepover mode.

No wonder they're tired.

It's easy to look at internet-connected people (and I'm not trying to suggest that it's only children) and say that they are playing on their phones all the time. They might be. They might also be connecting, feeling like they should be connecting, or longing to be connecting with someone on the other side.

We have an abundance of potential connections and no agreed-upon societal mores for how to deal with them. How long are we allowed to wait before we answer a text message? How do we tell people we are busy and not able to respond right now? How do we keep ourselves balanced and still make good connections with the people we love?

There are no correct answers to these questions. That's the most important thing to come to terms with. Part of the problem is that feeling that there is "a right way," that there is an answer out there somewhere, and we're just failing the test. We need to be able to talk to people about making decisions based on the best available information and choosing based on what we value.

Learning to talk about what we value and why might be the most important skill we need to get better at.

It's even more important now because many of the people we connect with online are not even in our local friendship groups. We don't necessarily have preestablished ideas of what we value. If we're not sure how to work our technology-mediated relationships with people we know and trust, how is it going to work with people we've never met? We are constantly consuming from or interacting with people who are not within our circle of knowledge. What do we do about it? What are the key points we need to understand?

Think about what so many have learned from Zoom in the last few years. We now talk about "Zoom fatigue." We've discovered that the time we spent walking in between meetings in our physical spaces was a really important time to collect ourselves. I'm increasingly seeing people shorten the traditional one-hour meeting to forty-five minutes, just to give us a chance to get our minds straight. We didn't consider walking around as "free time" before, but it seems to matter.

The gift of technology is the possibility of connection. We can potentially make the perfect connection that makes us less lonely. We can find the song lyrics. Or, potentially, we can find membership in a community that makes us feel special.

It's about belonging. People have always been lonely in one way or another. Where I certainly agree with Turkle is that we are losing our ability to be alone and embrace quiet. When we strive to belong at all costs, we can end up in strange places. Where we once felt like there must be no one else who felt the way we do, we can now reach out to an online community and find hundreds of others just like us. Or people we want to be like. Or people we will try to be like to feel like we belong.

Some people are taking advantage of this for their own purposes. They are taking on that Scholastic voice, the voice that knows the right answer, and it can sound like a clarion call. They present people with certainty, with clear narratives about what it means to belong, and it attracts people. We need to be suspicious of anyone who is providing 100 percent certainty on any complex issue. Being "sure" might be tempting, but as a goal, it's more likely to lead you to oversimplify an issue rather than come up with a workable approach going forward.

As our world diversifies, the communities held in my small town or in my country are no longer as easy to track and understand. The communities that we find and support are going to be increasingly important in the way we choose, whether that choice is about girls' soccer or how we should purchase things online.

We have connection. We can find community. But all the connections are available. And we can make all the communities, good and bad.

While we often associate learning with what happens in our schools, learning is something that is happening all the time. We learn how to be friends. We learn to help each other (or not). We learn to support a particular candidate because they are going to give us a lower tax rate (because "that's the smart way to do it").

We learn from each other. The community is the curriculum.

In a sense, it's always been that way. All those things that we learn in our textbooks are simply the ideas of other people who were fortunate enough to have the wealth, race, status, geography, and timing to make their thoughts worthy of being written down. They were still just people. The exclusiveness of those books meant that the curriculum we received, in my country at least, was predominantly male and predominantly white. That not only limits the number of people you are going to learn from, but it trains you to listen to a certain kind of voice and to accept a certain way of talking as the legitimate voice. One of the advantages/challenges of abundance is the rush of all those new voices. An advantage, certainly, that provides new ways for voices to be heard. A challenge for those who are accustomed to hearing a certain kind of story that matches their own.

It's hard to broaden your thinking. It upsets the balance and the comfort of how you currently think, particularly if you grew up with the freedom to do what you wanted to do. I was born with the privilege of having a dominant voice in my culture, which had nothing to do with whether I deserved to be listened to.

Think of the arguments people use against political correctness. "I need to watch everything I say." People who aren't in positions of privilege in our culture have *always* had to watch what they say. For those people with more power, they are being encouraged to watch what they say for the first time in their lives. It's work.

It forces you to realize that the ways you and your community think and act do not always match what you would like to think your values are.

How are we supposed to know what is currently the "correct" way to speak? Who gets to decide that? How can we learn about something we know nothing about if we don't know anything about it? What happens if someone gets angry when we do it wrong?

We have new challenges to deal with and new approaches we need to figure out.

We need to figure it out by talking to each other. By negotiating. By interacting and discussing. But that isn't easy either.

We all handle how we make connections in different ways. Some of us have the same friends we went to elementary school with and find connection in getting together and telling familiar stories. We find comfort in the expected. In the certain. Some of our connections are intensely activity-based, like music or fishing. Others spend their time with people from work.

Meeting people you know and have shared experiences with can be awesome, but how do we take those skills and use them in online communities?

When I got into online community learning in the mid-2000s, people still thought it was odd when I greeted someone

I had only met online as if we had been face-to-face friends for years.

"Where did you meet John?"

"Oh, we met on the internet."

For many years, "met on the internet" either meant that you connected on a dating app or that you were members of some subculture that was faintly embarrassing to talk about. If I tried to explain that John and I had worked on a podcast together, that might help a bit. But it still made for many awkward moments.

If you are one of these people who finds this odd, that's okay. Hang on through this part. You don't need to agree with me that making friends on the internet is a good idea. You just need to understand that *lots* of other people are doing it. We are finding groups of people to believe in. It's no different than the large swath of people who watch (and only watch) Fox News in the United States. They have found a thing to believe in. Online communities are like that, even if they are a bit harder to see or wrap your mind around.

One of the first things I learned facilitating online communities was how quickly an "us" can get constructed. In the same way that you can spend a weekend at a campground and become close friends with the people in the next tent, you can form very quick bonds of "we-ness" in an online community. You can suddenly find a group of people with a deep interest in gnome carving (literally something I do), and you can share knowledge and stories about your own carving that no one else has ever found interesting before. That's a great way to form friendships.

The abundance of connection available online means that, if you can find an ongoing conversation with people like you, the first hurdle to making a connection is out of the way. If you searched for this community, you used keywords that reflected your interests. If I search for "why beavers are bad," and I find a community of beaver haters, we already have a shared belief that allows our connection to grow.

If we are already thinking the same things, we have a point of bonding and something to talk about right away. Text-based relationships also have the huge advantage of being asynchronous or semi-asynchronous. In a discussion forum like Reddit, you might be responding to a post from several hours, days, or even weeks ago. This can give you lots of opportunities to write the perfect response, which may involve a Google search for the perfect analogy or quote from a movie. A semi-synchronous space, like a text chat you're having on your phone or online, still allows you to filter the thoughts that pop into your head. It gives you a chance to hit the back button and try wording that joke in a slightly better way. It also gives you an opportunity to *not* weigh in without creating an awkward silence.

Online connection can be great. But there are several side effects that can be difficult to track.

The group of people you're meeting online and the connections between them will often be making their own meaning. They will be making memories together based on things people have said, just like that group of friends from high school who you still see in the summer. Things become true to the people inside the group because they are believed in the group. This is a process that used to take a long time. We talked a few chapters ago about how common practices on the telephone emerged as we went along. Some of those practices may not even apply anymore (saying your name when you introduce yourself on the phone in a world of caller ID), but they are important parts of how we interact with each other. They are the social glue of our relationships.

With an online community, those decisions about how we act tend to get made quickly. They are often an extension of the default practices of the founders of those communities, or sometimes, they are practices that emerge based on the people who have joined. Those practices could extend to anything. In our earlier Wikipedia examples, the commonly accepted practice is that if you have a fact claim, you need to cite a published reference. In other communities, only information that comes from "community-approved sources" will be accepted. If those sources have malicious intent, the community will likely start to believe inaccurate or misleading things. People will make meaning, and they will choose what to believe based on the choices made in their communities. They will learn their community.

To those of us outside of the flat-earther movement, the idea of a flat earth might seem ridiculous. Inside the movement, *everyone* believes that the earth is flat. Reinforcement for that belief is everywhere. All arguments against what other people believe are common in the conversation. I'm sure they have jokes about how gullible the rest of us are. And they belong. They belong to an "us." They are Flat-Earthers.

The common response here is that we are not so gullible. We choose to believe the things we choose to believe. Maybe. But all our knowledge is founded on the thinking of other people: scientists, philosophers, charlatans, or bombasts. Our beliefs have to come from somewhere.

Our face-to-face world made the spread of ideas limited. It was limited to how many times we could get together. It was limited to the region of the world you lived in. Your beaver-hating society might have had a magazine and pamphlets, but you were still limited by both the practical realities of distribution and the simple fact that paper things are hard to find.

Now, these communities of belief are happening everywhere. They are happening outside of us, surely, but they are happening to each of us too. As the world changes more quickly and as so many new ideas pop up, we too are finding our "places to believe." These are places that allow us to feel like we belong. They are, often, places where you will find *right answers*. Some of those things we believe are, you know, just wrong. And some of them are dangerously wrong.

Let's take a commonly held belief that I had until recently. The story goes like this. In the future, a large percentage of occupations will not be the jobs that are being done today. Space car driver. Wind farm technician. There will be tons of jobs that don't even exist now, and *we* must do something about it. This argument is generally followed by the idea that we need to teach people how to learn because we can't actually train them for the jobs they are going to have in the future (since we don't know what those jobs are going to be).

I believed this. Not in an "I'm going to plan for a new future job" kind of way, but I repeated it to other people. I thought of it as accepted knowledge because I heard it a lot.

I had heard, through a variety of means, that jobs in the future were going to be different than the jobs that we have now. We have a whole new version of this with the coming of AI systems that can replicate the writing of humans. All the jobs that involve writing will disappear. We'll all be AI programmers, or something. I mean, that stands to reason. We're not all farmers or soldiers anymore. We already covered that we don't have telephone operators like we used to. I know a lot of people who are making a living doing jobs that didn't exist when they were in school. Sure, jobs are going to be different in the future.

That level of uncertainty is unsettling enough, but there are usually numbers that are attached to this theory. The most common set of numbers seems to show that in the next fifteen years, two-thirds of the jobs are going to be different. Holy. We'd better do something about this *right now*.

It's not a big leap from "Hey, some jobs are going to be different" to believing the numbers that are associated with it. Someone must have researched it right? A quick Google search shows that lots of respectable people seem to be using those numbers.

My eyes were opened to the history of the "future of work" narrative in a blog post by Benjamin Doxtdator, a middle school educator living in Belgium. It's a well-cited article written by a Canadian and a member of the Oneida nation. Doxtdator has an established online presence and is connected inside various educational communities that I participate in. I trust his voice. When you read his other work, what you see is a thoughtful and passionate educator. His voice is not one that I would have heard before the internet.

In his blog post, Doxtdator tracks the history of the "future of work" narrative back to 1957 when people said that in the future, people will be doing jobs that no one now even knows about. And people just kept saying it. Various versions of "In fifteen years, 65 percent of the jobs that people are going to be doing don't exist now." It became such a common expression that serious educational organizations started saying it. It's circular citation. Once one reasonable person says it as if it's true, lots of people start saying it. Everyone has "cited" each other, but there is no original source. The future jobs thing, uh, hasn't happened. It probably won't happen. I mean, you could argue that it might happen in the next fifteen years. I can't prove that that isn't true. I can tell you that for people who said it fifteen years ago, it hasn't happened. Sure, there are new jobs, but nowhere near 65 percent of jobs.

Whoa now, why are we trusting a blog post instead of the work that was published by some major international organization or something that appears in books by "thought leaders" like Thomas Friedman? Well, Doxtdator tracks the story of the sources for one. It's easy for someone coming from a large multinational organization to simply talk about things they think might happen. The old predictions clearly didn't stand the test of time. We are fortunate to be able to look back and see that they didn't, in fact, happen. We can also see that the argument isn't actually based on anything. It's a story with far-reaching impacts.

Ideas spread. In this case, when you read through Doxtdator's blog post, these ideas were spread by mostly well-meaning people who had read about something, thought it made sense, and in many cases, tried to do something about all these jobs changing because they thought they should.

Okay. Got it. Don't trust reputable organizations, and don't trust experts.

Suddenly, I become the reason we can't have nice things.

But this is what happens, right? As soon as we find that someone has made a mistake, we start to not trust the entirety of the system. I went looking to an organization for a *right answer*, didn't find it, and now all organizations are lying. If you add a community of people who are going around finding other predictions amidst uncertainty that turned out to be wrong, you've got yourself a dangerous little community that doesn't believe in anyone but themselves.

Or, alternately, we no longer care if a person or organization makes mistakes or misrepresents truth. We listen to them anyway. Neither of these outcomes makes for a healthy, functional, and caring society. It also makes for a life of constant disappointment.

The process of making meaning in an information-abundant society is uncertain. We need to understand the information that we are presented with. We need to understand the people who created that information or, more likely, the people who recycled that information. We have thousands of issues just like the future jobs example that we need to make decisions about. How can we do that and retain our sanity?

We need to do all that *and* make good decisions.

A piece of research done by Justin Dellinger during his tenure with the LINK Research Lab at the University of Texas at Arlington does a nice job of illustrating the challenge faced by many of us in our professional lives. He interviewed educational leaders in northern Texas and asked them how they made decisions about the technologies they used at a system level.

It turns out that the leaders in Dellinger's research tended to not read the research that was written by subject matter experts regarding technology. We could make any number of assumptions about this, but even asking people in an interview why they don't read something is no guarantee of a useful answer. It could be that they find the research ineffective, impractical, or unreadable, but it's likely that they would not give this answer. The research might be difficult to find. It might be "too long" to read. One way or the other, they aren't reading it.

In addition to this, the leaders suggested they also did not believe the vendors of the software who visited them. They saw those presentations for what they were: a glossed-up version of the software that neither reflects the total costs over the lifetime of the project nor the reality of instructional benefits in real-world situations. Often the salespeople don't even know how the software works after it is sold. That kind of support is handled by a different part of the company.

So, I don't read the research about it, and I don't believe the people selling it. What do I do? Well, I look around at what everyone else in my field is doing, and I copy the piece that seems to make the most sense. The internet makes this super easy. Pop on over to the technology plan for another district, read through what they've got in there, and integrate it into your plan.

Only, they probably did the same. We are left to wonder who wrote the first plan that the first district copied from. I'm not in any way trying to suggest that people simply copy other people's plans, but in the dozen or so educational strategy projects I've been involved in, I have yet to be in one where a senior person doesn't say, "Hey, let's look at what _____ are doing." Truth be told, the easiest way to get your part of the plan approved is often to show that it's already in someone else's plan.

Reading someone's strategy from the internet can be helpful to a point, but it leaves aside all the negotiations that happened inside the organization before that document was completed. You don't know what challenges the organization decided to keep internal. You don't know what horse trading went on to get a piece added. You are lacking the context, and without that context, it's tough to make a good decision.

This is true of all these decisions we make. It's a fight for the context. The information machine that is the internet is good to serve up all kinds of information, and we need to be constantly looking for the context. We need to look for other possible answers. We need to be asking ourselves why the person who wrote this information wrote it the way that they did.

We need to accept that there are no right answers to complex questions. Just because most of the jobs people will be doing in fifteen years already exist doesn't mean we shouldn't still be prepared to make change. Just because there are concussions in girls' soccer doesn't mean we should stop playing. When we stop seeing the complexity of these issues, when we simplify important things in our lives for the sake of the time it takes to think about them, we make mistakes.

Trust. And verify.

Humbly.

And we need it. We need a new way to think about what is valuable to us and what we are going to choose to believe. Our own abundance of information is starting to affect the world around us in ways that are difficult to understand. Aren't we better off with more information?

We are stuck. We are stuck in our old approaches.

In an expert-driven world where we believe what is written in important books, it is easier to get everyone to do the same things. Our epistemology, here in a space of information abundance, seems to be tied to our identity. We believe that meaning is made by believing the people who are part of the world that we want to believe in.

I'm happy to follow the scientific consensus on a given topic as far as I can. I do think that the checks and balances that are in place at most institutions (e.g., research ethics boards, grant reviews, peer reviews) will catch most mistakes the majority of the time. It's not a perfect model, but believing in consensus science certainly seems better to me than the alternative.

That alternative always seems to include some kind of conspiracy where thousands of people have all worked to hide some valuable piece of evidence or mislead us for their own purposes. Individuals or single companies can do this. Large, disconnected groups can barely organize themselves to figure out where to have dinner, let alone cleverly orchestrate an international conspiracy. I've done too much project management to believe in conspiracies.

So, whose responsibility is it to do something about it? Go ahead. Look to your left and right and see if there's someone there who is going to be in charge of the change we need. In an age of information abundance, you can't find the right consultant or researcher to tell you how we need to change ourselves to be happy and have hope.

You can remember how things were when you were a child and how people used to talk to each other. You can bemoan the way you only see people sitting with phones at tables and not even looking at each other. You could quit Facebook because it's a cesspool and Twitter because it's full of trolls. You could do all of that, but most people would still be there, and if you consider yourself to be a reasonable person, you're taking one more reasonable person off the platform who could influence it for the better.

It takes each person making little changes in their lives in a way that supports the things we value. Every time we make an effort to challenge a malicious fact and every time we engage in polite conversation with someone we disagree with, we impact "the way things should be done."

In a world of information abundance, we are the curriculum for everyone else. Every time we post something, every time we retweet it, every time we choose to comment prosaically on someone's work, we are teaching everyone else how to be, how to think, and what to think.

We have so many choices and so much information. We just aren't equipped for it. We were trained to confront questions with answers. To look for certainty.

And it's hurting us.

CHAPTER 6

Learning to Confront Uncertainty

A funny thing happened on the way to writing this book. I had imagined myself pulling together sixteen years of blog posts and more years of teaching and, well, living and putting some kind of story together. It would be the culmination of many years of mistakes, work, and conversations, my attempt to have a long conversation about some of the things I care about. A story about learning in a time of abundance.

I had it all sorted in my mind . . . and then the pandemic happened.

Before the pandemic, I saw uncertainty as something that was lurking beneath the surface for many. The more privileged you were, the less uncertainty you saw. But, I was going to argue, it was hiding underneath many of the challenges we faced every day in a culture blessed/burdened with information abundance. Then the uncertainty took over entirely.

Since February of 2020, everyone has been confronted by the uncertainty of science and scientists, who have been doing their best to give us advice about how to put masks over our mouths, about how close we should be to one another. We've been confronted with masses of information about the varying impacts of different versions of a vaccine. For a while, I was washing my groceries before I put them away or the kids touched them. A lot happened, and like so many others, I wasn't sure what I was doing most of the time. Living in Windsor, Ontario, Canada, I listened to the news on the blockade at the US border by anti-maskers. I also got long COVID and didn't know if I was going to be able to keep my job or, frankly, finish this book.

I got lucky in one way during the pandemic though. I had the distinct pleasure of working with about eighty students during their co-op work term. With the coming of the pandemic, many of the positions that those students had lined up with companies in engineering, business, kinesiology, and computer science dried up. Those students unexpectedly ended up working with a learning specialist who works on digital strategy. (That's me.)

This group changed my perspective on the relationship between how we teach in schools and how prepared students are for a world full of uncertainty.

My lesson hinges on one simple story. In the middle of a meeting, two weeks into one work term, a student interrupted me in the middle of a project meeting and said, "Dave, I think I have to apologize to you."

The student was a polite, hardworking engineering student who had never been a problem and showed clear signs of intelligence and creativity. He continued, "It's just that you've been asking me for my opinion for the last two weeks, and I . . . I thought you were lying. No adult has ever asked my opinion before and not already known what answer they wanted. I realized today that when you ask me for my opinion, you actually want it."

And that's when it all came together for me. The way we look at learning. The way we teach people to learn. The way that my students had learned how to learn. For them, learning was about getting the right answer. They thought the only way to respond to a question was to, somehow, give the right answer. They had determined that learning followed a pattern:

1. People ask me questions that have right answers.
2. The person asking the question knows the answer.
3. I'm going to be judged on my ability to give them the right answer.

They had learned that there's no room for nuance. No room for them to apply their values to the conversation. No room for the complexity of real life. Is it any wonder that students struggle when we ask them to think for themselves? They certainly can think for themselves, but they've been specifically taught that those thoughts are not what people are looking for.

Michelene Chi and Robert Glaser are two educational researchers from the '80s who used a nice distinction that I've found helpful when thinking about my students and their ability to make decisions. In their work "Problem-Solving Ability," published in 1985, these researchers made a separation between "classroom problems" and "real-life problems" (7).

A classroom problem is one where you have a clear problem, a clear method for solving the problem, and a verifiable answer. Classroom problems are great for teaching us the algorithm for answering well-defined problems. How do I stop my tap from leaking? Tighten the bolt, change the O-ring, or replace the tap. Those are all clear approaches to solving the problem. And the result? My tap doesn't leak. I can measure that. There's a right answer. There's an observable outcome.

That approach is totally fine for problems we can solve. Math problems, temperature problems, assembling an IKEA shelf (maybe). Any problem that has a counting noun that we can use to determine whether we have succeeded. I'm cold. Turn up the temperature. Oh, look, the temperature has gone up. I am no longer cold. I have solved my problem.

But what about when we're trying to solve a problem that doesn't have a solution? What if I'm interested in supporting creativity? What if I'm trying to encourage independence? Or kindness? You might say, "Well, those are things that we learn outside the classroom. That's not a teacher's job."

Maybe. But we are all, at some point, responsible for the kindness of the people around us. We demonstrate our perspectives on kindness or empathy or toughness or a thousand other characteristics in our daily actions, which can all be seen by other people. We also, I would argue, need to make sure that when people learn to address the problems around them in places like a school, we encourage them to use values like climate awareness or empathy in their decision-making process.

We are the curriculum of what it means to be part of our community. We learn what it means to be in a community by watching the community.

The things that we deal with in our communities can be difficult. They are often problems that we've had for a long time. Problems that are difficult to get our minds around. Problems that are frustrating to think about. Problems that are easier, frankly, to not think about.

In 1973 Horst Rittel and Melvin Webber wrote what might be my favorite piece of writing about problems. It's called "Dilemmas in a General Theory of Planning." Snappy title, I know.

In it they talk about "wicked problems" (160). Wicked problems have no clear solutions. Each problem is likely the symptom of another problem. Sometimes there's no way to even formulate the problem properly. You have to oversimplify the problem to even talk about it. This is the opposite of what Chi and Glaser called a classroom problem. These are real-life problems. The problems you and I have.

Take the "I'm cold and need to turn up the heat" example from earlier. There are a number of complicating factors in that example when you start to think about it. Every time I turn up the heat in my house instead of, say, putting on a sweater, I burn more fossil fuels. I might not choose to turn up the heat for other reasons. It could be that I'm worried about being able to pay the heating bill, or I might not be a person who has control of the temperature in the place that I live. From a privileged perspective, many of those uncertainties are invisible, but they are still there.

And just because we can't "solve" wicked problems doesn't mean we don't have to do something about them. We have to decide about soccer. We have to help our kids (and ourselves) handle our devices. We still need to make (or buy) the pasta sauce.

We've established that if we're dealing with a classroom-style problem, using a problem-solving method is a perfectly reasonable approach. Choose a design challenge. Or a nice tidy problem that someone can solve and we're good. Your cat is hungry. Feed your cat. Problem solved.

But we all know that we have problems that don't define themselves so easily. And just because we can't define them doesn't mean we can't make them better. The housing crisis, for example, is different everywhere and for everyone. I hear people my age privileged enough to own a house talking about the value of their houses as if the crisis has been a good thing. Most of the students I work with never expect to be able to buy a house, nor do they know where they're going to live. More troubling, in Detroit, across the border from where I live, whole communities were identified as dangerous because they had predominantly black populations. This racial profiling, called redlining, meant that people of color struggled to get loans for buying houses or struggled to sell their houses, and this practice still impacts the rights of people in the city today.

And, from my own perspective, how does my privilege around having a house affect the overall system? I don't understand the economy well enough to recognize my own place in it, but what do I tell my kids and the students I work with about their future? What should I be doing in my community to help people who aren't housed in healthy and safe ways? How much of the public narrative around housing is being controlled by people who have a vested interest in the housing market being out of control?

Some of these questions have answers. There is data.

But every single question leads you down ten different roads. Every time you think you have an answer, you're ripe for someone to come along and give you another piece of information (made-up or real) that makes that approach uncertain. If you consider age discrimination, have you left out issues of race or socioeconomic status? We can't ever "solve" the problem. We can only ever work on parts, learn about new parts, and then try to work on those.

Think of the other examples in this book. How do we teach our children and ourselves to use these new technologies we have? How do we decide to use new medical discoveries about concussions to impact our choices about sports? How do we decide to choose the foods we should eat?

Now think a little farther back to all the conversations we've had in the last twenty years about vaccines. Think about voting. Think about the ways in which companies are trying to sell us a way of living, to turn us into brands.

These are the real decisions that make up our lives.

There is no right way to decide. There are, I would suggest, probably lots of bad ways to go, but they are decisions that live in uncertainty.

It's not that we didn't have uncertainty before the internet. We had it before we had an abundance of information at our fingertips. Things have always been uncertain to some degree. Ask a farmer what uncertainty looks like. Or a wood carver approaching a new piece of wood. Or a parent trying to decide whether their kid should go to their first unsupervised party.

In the past, however, most of the uncertainty was hidden from us. By the time the food came to our table or we bought the beautiful wooden bowl or we met someone's kid, we saw a finished product. All concerns about the weather, weird grains in the wood, and a scared kid wanting to fit in were invisible to us. Before the internet, we mostly encountered finished products with all the uncertainty handled by someone else.

We've looked at the way learning has been structured for thousands of years. For much of our history, we were trading in certainty. If we were trying to get people to learn letters or the meaning of words or to remember certain pieces of vital information or memorize books that they couldn't afford, we needed a final product, a certainty, in order for us to remember the information that we needed.

And so we've gotten used to certainty. But if we're going to get the "right" answer, someone out there has to be able to tell us what the answer actually is. Someone has to know, and we have to believe them. And that works fine if there is an answer to the question. What are the molecules that make up water? What is the capital of New Zealand (still not Auckland)? What is the square root of twenty-five?

But as for those other things, we've relied on tradition and habit and people in positions of authority to tell us what the answer is. We've inherited our "common" sense. We ate the foods we were given or could find. We took care of our lawns. We got our polio vaccines.

But now. Now we have access to all the uncertainty behind those decisions. In some cases, that shared common sense has shown itself to be a perspective on things that is shared by small controlled communities, not by the population at large. As different communities come together, we can see how what we thought of as common sense only worked when access to power and voice was heavily restricted to the few.

We know now that when it comes to food, it depends. We know that watering our lawns uses a lot of water and might not be a terribly good idea in some places. We know that vaccines (while amazing and world-changingly good) were the product of lots of people working hard and getting better and better at something, not a magical got-it moment where it was suddenly perfect.

Things like science, it turns out, aren't magic. I mean, scientists have been telling us that for years, but we didn't have access to the information to prove it. Even the marketing on TV has been telling us that "four of five doctors agree" for generations, but it still hasn't sunk in that professionals are not in perfect agreement with one another on all issues. Most of them are people doing their best, with the best information available, to make the best choices amid uncertainty. They are, each of them, affected by their biases toward the different people who come into their offices. Even among global leaders in various research fields, universal truths are difficult to come by.

Now we have access to much of the same information that they do. All the unfinished products of science. All the different recipes for making bread. All the pundits telling us how we should be using our phones. All the parenting advice in the world.

To butcher an old phrase, we need the knowledge to know fact from uncertainty and the wisdom to know whether we should be weighing in on that uncertainty.

Because if there's an underused twenty-first-century literacy, it's humility. The humility to look at a situation, at a piece of science, at a conflict in another part of the world that we have no expertise on and say, "I will not chime in on this." Simply replying, "I don't know" to the issue of the day, whether at the watercooler or on a Facebook post, is maybe the most important response we can give.

And humility doesn't necessarily need to lead to inaction. It just means that your having some—almost always partial—information does not make you someone from whom others should be learning. Reading is not, in and of itself, research. And your information does not trump lived experience and impact.

I live in Canada. It has a history (continuing into the present) of terrible colonial violence and mistreatment of Indigenous peoples. Land was stolen and appropriated through often-underhanded treaties. Children were systematically removed from their homes and cultures for generations as part of an abusive residential school system overtly created in service of assimilation and white supremacy. In 2015, the country's Truth and Reconciliation Commission published ninety-four calls to action, both to raise awareness of these harmful legacies and to propose real steps for reconciliation.

I have read the recommendations, with my own children, as part of a Canada Day public reading aimed at shifting the way that national "holiday" is marked. I can know all of this and teach it. But as a white descendant of settlers, I know not only am I *not* an expert on Indigenous Canada, but I am also part of the fabric of the power structure that impedes reconciliation. So, who I amplify and defer to in conversations that are fundamentally not mine to define is important.

Debunking a racist trope in a public space? That can be a good use of my (loud) voice. Other conversations about indigeneity may go further if I don't chime in, or at least if I don't assume I should.

We don't always know in advance what conversations we're entering or who we're addressing, especially online. That space of uncertainty is an invitation to reflection: What is my responsibility here? Who am I addressing? What authority am I exerting or reinforcing?

Abundance constantly confronts us with whether our contributions to the world serve to make it better for those we share it with. All the inequalities of our culture, good and bad, still apply. Research tells us that résumés with traditionally female names get fewer call-backs. The same goes for names that people identify as racialized in some way.

And because we do have so many choices, it's often overwhelming. We can, certainly, do our reading in some cases, like when we're trying to decide which dishwasher to buy, and deal with some of the choices we face. Some of the time. There are things that are structured enough, in one way or another, for us to choose.

Other things simply aren't. I am never going to know enough about climate science to make a "decision" or "do the research" to the point where I am going to be able to clearly evaluate what's happening. I need help. I need to find shortcuts to get me there. I need to find a trusted source. Access to information (for those who even have access) is no solution to our social ills by itself. It does, however, lead to the need for a reordering of the skills we should be developing.

Which brings us to our second twenty-first-century literacy: informed trust.

Democracies are designed for us to vote for a representative to make our decisions. That person, ostensibly, is going to take their time hiring other people who know what we should do about carbon credits or sewer lines under our streets or bicycle lanes, and that person is going to make better decisions for us, right? Well, that's how it's supposed to work anyway. Representative democracy. That's an expression of trust.

But now those elected officials have a day-to-day idea of what the electorate wants on a given issue. Every time we comment on something, every time we take a position that someone else can track, we are influencing the decisions that get made for us. We influence our government in terms of what they think people want, and we influence the companies who are trying to get us to buy things.

When we speak, we affect what decisions get made. When we speak after we've been influenced by misinformation or disinformation, someone is using us to affect what decisions get made.

We can try to control the internet by making sure that everything that gets put there is checked by someone (which has not been very effective so far), *or* we can help people do a better job dealing with uncertainty.

The attempt to control speech in public spaces is something that we've worked on many times before. The newspaper is basically an attempt at doing that. Although newspapers used to be more overtly politically aligned, at least you knew from the beginning what you were getting into. Now newspapers still have political leanings, though they're more often implied than written in the header. Many of us have a sense of what part of the political/thought spectrum a particular newspaper comes from, and we include that in our understanding of what we read. The brand of the newspaper gives us the context we need to understand the perspective of a given author.

Those newspapers have changed a great deal over the last fifteen years. Fifteen years ago, we bought a newspaper. We bought the whole thing. You might not have liked the sports section or the cartoons, or you might not have cared about international issues, but you got it in the newspaper anyway. Those sections of the newspaper weren't trying to reach you directly. They were there for the people who wanted them. If you were writing a story for that paper, you might have heard whether some people liked it or disliked it, but it was part of the whole paper. Readers trusted the whole newspaper, or they didn't.

Now the readership of each article is tracked using analytics. Each newspaper story gets an audience, and we know exactly how many people read it and for how long. Instead of there being one lead story in a paper that is meant to attract people's attention on the street corner, each story has the ability to gather attention. Each story has to have an attention-grabbing title and content so that readers will choose it from all the different options that are out there on the internet.

Now we need to know the perspective of the author of the article instead of just the newspaper. We need to create our sense of informed trust directly with the individual writing the story. As AI writing tools continue to develop, we'll need to be on the look out for those as well. Is that author even a person? Is this someone who can be trusted to do their own work? Do I know anyone that I trust who can verify this information?

In high school, we were (and still are) told that we needed to use a credible source for citation in our essays. If we were going to choose a book, we had to know the publisher and the year it was published (also the city it was published in, though I can't say I know why). If a book had been published, that meant that somebody was willing to spend the money on publishing it. The publisher put its name on the book, and that meant that the publisher was putting its name/brand behind the author. The date would tell us how long ago the source was written so that we knew how up-to-date the information was.

Those were the tools that we had. But did any of us really know one publisher from another? Was the average person going to know anything about an author and their actual expertise in the field they were writing about? These methods of establishing trust were designed to help people who were expert enough to recognize a publisher or an author. A level of expertise that none of us, practically, will ever attain, certainly not in more than a few fields.

So, what should our "academic" papers look like now? Should we still be doing the same things to discover the authenticity of the things that we are reading? Maybe a more important question: Should we ever have done it that way? Was the research paper from 1985 simply the best we could do in an information-scarcity situation, or was it good practice?

Well, if you believe that an academic paper is necessary because we need to learn how to write an academic paper in college, I guess I'm forced to agree with you. We do use cited academic essays in college, but are they still necessary to prepare people for life or for the workforce? Given the advancements in generative writing software, very few people are going to be writing long-form text from scratch in their work lives. They'll be using an AI system for creating an outline, hopefully editing it for content, and submitting it. I'm not looking forward to this world, but it is so much quicker, that I find it difficult to believe that we won't be seeing it. I'm not saying no one is going to write long-form. I'm just suggesting that it's not really going to be that common.

Any writing that follows a pattern like an essay or a report—that is essentially an algorithm—can be done by machine. New machine-based tools like GPT-4 are now doing such a good job imitating human writing that they are able to answer essay questions in a mostly readable and "human" way. They're not perfect, but they are able to follow a process. They can repeat the algorithm of "literature review." It doesn't matter how much you want something like writing a précis or a literature review to be an important skill that people need to know, tasks like these are now done by computers.

Those AI systems have deeply problematic biases in the way they create text. Because they are built on source text from the internet, that source text informs the writing automatically. It could include any bias that you could find on the internet. The generated texts are also boring. Really boring. They are the autotune of writing. The AI systems are designed to make the blandest text possible.

Those old research skills were designed to save us from the nonsense that was published in disreputable paper sources. They were designed to force students to "read the work" so that the teacher had some expectation that the student was doing the work of learning to find information in a library, reading through books, and finding reliable opinions. Every student now has access to a website that can perform a written reply or a basic essay in seconds.

How do we understand the skills needed to deal with the information sources that are confronting us today? How do we inform ourselves about CBD oil or GMO products or about how we can make our houses more environmentally friendly? How does our society understand how to sift through all the propaganda and silliness to make an informed decision?

And it matters if people are informed. We saw earlier how people are using the technologies of abundance to shape our democracy. We need to change the way we learn to fight against the people and organizations who are trying to skew our impressions and our votes to serve their agendas.

How can we learn to make better decisions about the world around us when we are confronted with so much information and so many people trying to manipulate our position? How can we learn to understand and accept/challenge the decisions of those who have, for one reason or another, gotten the right to make decisions for us in our society?

Along with humility and informed trust, I'll make a pitch for one more literacy for the twenty-first century: the ability to apply our values to decision making. We need to understand how everyone's practices (including our own) are full of hidden values that we've accrued over the years. To see how we can take implicit assumptions and make them explicit to allow us to make useful, sustainable change in our lives. And that can be hard. That desire to find the evidence, to find the "right" way to do it can be difficult to overcome.

But we need to bring those values up to the surface and ask ourselves what is important to us, particularly when one of the things influencing our feelings on something is a vague feeling of discomfort.

I, for instance, have a terrible situational memory. Oh, I can remember the date of something that happened 1,500 years ago and tell you about it. But if you've made it this far into this book, you might have guessed that already. I struggle when it comes to remembering specific things in a given moment. Like someone's name. Because of this, I am all about saying things like "that woman we met" and "that guy with the hair."

But I have learned, in the last few years, to define people in ways that don't simply refer to my own perception of their gender. I have started to change my unconscious phrases from "that woman who" or "that guy who" as a way of describing people to gender-neutral phrases, like "the person we met at the park." And in struggling to change that practice, I can end up not knowing what to say. (My memory is really quite terrible, but it's not like it keeps me awake at night.) This small change that happens everyday can be difficult to adjust to. The uncertainty of what I'm supposed to do can be upsetting.

But when I sat down and thought about my use of pronouns, my values were clear. People can define themselves as they like. I like to make people feel welcome. I am happy to respect people's choices about themselves, as long as they don't directly infringe on other people's choices (broadly speaking, most of the time). And, clearly, other people's self-definition doesn't infringe on anyone. Spelled out like that, the effort to get around my gender-naming habits seems totally worthwhile.

I recognize that my values on this aren't universal. But I wonder how many people, like me, are more uncomfortable with not knowing what they are supposed to do than they are offended by something that has nothing to do with them. "Well, I know what a woman is" or "We have always been like this" feels like an appeal to certainty as much as it feels like an appeal to some set of values.

We feel a sense of discomfort when uncertainty comes around. A sense of being unsettled. We are not able to draw on our existing templates to deal with the problem, so, too often, we reach out for certainty. It's a defense mechanism. A nice warm blanket of being right.

And, too often, that certainty comes out to the other person as hate, as dismissal, as a lack of acceptance. We need to be able to help people sit inside that uncertainty and learn to care more for the person in front of them than they care for their own discomfort.

This world of abundance of connection means we are going to encounter lots of people who are outside of our lived experience, which is why we need humility, informed trust, and values.

In a world where we can reach out for the opinions and information of so many people, we should start most of our learning with the same question: Is this uncertain? If you need simple information, no problem. What is the capital of Iran? These kinds of fact-based questions are awesome. The internet is wonderful for this. Facts are important. There are many good strategies out there for establishing whether things that can be true are true.

This book, though, is about the things that we can't or won't ever know for certain. They are questions that leave us with answers like, "It depends." When you look at the way people talk about learning, you'll often hear them use examples like math or remembering the answers to questions that have clear outcomes. "Kids these days can't even do their times tables" or "Research says that students learn better when they memorize."

For what it's worth, that's probably true. If you memorize your times tables, you'll, you know, remember them. But if you want to know how to become a better parent or who you should vote for, you'll find that you'll get different answers from different people. There is no "best parent" award with a list of actions that the parent took. I take that back, there probably are a thousand of them, each with a different list. Each parent is parenting a different child in a different situation, in a different culture with different goals and values that affect what might be a good decision at any given time. If you think about it, a lot of things in our world are like this.

We could probably come up with a list of things that a parent shouldn't do. And that's an important caveat. Even in conversations that are difficult to figure out, there are always things participants can decide are off the table. There's some consensus that can be reached in almost every problem. And just because there is a gray area, that doesn't mean that all gray areas are created equal.

The solution to uncertainty is not always to find "certainty." This doesn't mean that there is nothing we know or understand but that the goal of dealing with uncertainty is not to find "the answer." That's where things usually fall apart. But the solution is not to just do whatever either. We organize our values, think deeply about how we trust, and humbly walk into the problem, knowing all we can do is our best.

If we look at all the wicked problems around us, they are problems that we will always be working on. There is probably no "solution" to poverty, but we could improve the plight of some people, in some ways, some of the time. If we work hard on it, it might be a lot of people. If we imagine these problems as having solutions, we're bound for disappointment. There's no finish, no stop. We have values that we work to support when we can. We are going to need to see that as our goal if we're going to be happy in this world, where we can see so much of the good and so much of the terrible.

All we can do is share our stories, our thinking, and our perspectives in ways that can help one another. We can share our hope that while things won't be the best, they can get better. We need to be the best curriculum we can be.

CHAPTER 7

Practices for an Abundant World

Pick a word. Any word. Go look at its dictionary definition. Now, ask yourself if that definition represents the whole story of that word. It doesn't matter if the word you pick is *table* or *poverty*, it's likely that the definition is not going to encompass everything you know or, more importantly, everything everyone else knows about that word. But that definition does offer a place to start, which is helpful. If you think back to our conversation about the schools in Mesopotamia, you'll remember that they were developing the basis of the written language. They needed to standardize. Desperately. A place to start can be important.

I've been in a lot of arguments over the *real* definition of words over the years. Pretty sure that doesn't say great things about me. I eventually learned, after an embarrassingly long time, that a large chunk of those arguments resulted from a lack of shared premises. Take, for example, the word *learning*. As with so many uncertain topics, there are things I'm comfortable saying learning *doesn't* mean. But when I think of the ways I've talked about learning in this book, there are a lot of meanings that aren't encompassed by any definition that I've ever seen. There are lots of other ways to understand *learning* that mean something to you that I haven't talked about at all or don't understand. Anytime we define something, we inevitably exclude things from that definition. And anytime we accept someone else's definition, we often don't see what they have chosen to exclude or, more importantly, why.

So much of what many of us did when we "learned" stuff before abundance was to learn a shorthand. When we were asked to "learn" things that were certain, we were given a "truth" and told to remember it. I still remember the Bohr model of the atom I had to memorize for my chemistry class. I have come to understand that it significantly oversimplifies what an atom looks like and has been obsolete for decades. Scientific understandings have become more complex; representations have improved. That is literally how science works. We move, hopefully, toward less uncertainty or, at least, to a better-explained uncertainty. But the Bohr model is still taught in schools.

Putting a complex concept in a simplified package makes it easier to carry around. And that's helpful. But having that little shorthand about how a piece of science works should not become us "believing" in a thing without thinking about it. One of the great, powerful things about uncertainty is it allows us to grow. If we become too sure of ourselves and our definitions, too caught up in our own way of seeing things, we can't make space for new things or new perspectives. We can't adapt. We can't understand someone else who isn't like us. I see your table, it doesn't look like my table, and I think it's weird.

We use shorthand for those things that aren't very important to us, as well as for things outside our realm of expertise.

I don't know if the emergency fire escape plan posted in a building is genuinely the best way to get out of a particular fire. There could be a tiger down a hallway that the fire marshal wasn't anticipating when they designed the plan. But we need a shorthand for fire exits so that there's some chance for survival, most of the time.

In twenty-or-so years of working on change in learning, one of the most important rules I've learned is to never ask anyone for their opinion on something they aren't likely to know about. Which fire exit is the right one? What email system should my campus use? What's the best kind of exercise? How do you, a parent, think students should learn math? These kinds of questions are filled with deep complexities and differing levels of expertise. But if you ask someone, they feel like they should know. Asking the question suggests there is an answer. Asking *them* suggests *they* should know the answer. So, they answer, and then they attach to that answer, even if they don't know any more about the issue than they did before they responded.

If writing this book has taught me anything, it's to say, "I don't know" more often. Not "I don't care about what you're saying. Stop asking." Rather, "I don't know enough to really have an opinion, but this is how this issue affects me." Or, even, "This is the person I think does know about this thing, and I trust them."

We still need to have functional ways of replying to questions that are *obviously* outside our realm of expertise but are about issues on which we need or want to weigh in. I've had to decide multiple times during the writing of this book whether I should send my kid to school in the middle of a pandemic. I'm not an epidemiologist. But I've still had to choose.

It's critical that we transition from trying to find the right answer to trying to find the best answer for right now. We need to move from thinking we are "solving" a problem to dealing with that problem. That way of thinking is not as satisfying in the short term. We don't get to cross the problem off the list.

Understanding that our problems are not things that can be solved is less dispiriting in the long run, though. For so many of our questions, we are never going to have all the data, we're never going to have the perfect framing, or, maybe what's most difficult, we'll never have anyone to tell us that we did the right thing.

Accepting that there isn't a right answer can be a humbling process. You need to sort your values and decide what's important to you. Then you need to decide who and what you're going to trust. Knowing that we're never going to be sure about our decisions from the start and still trying to do our best is often the best we can do.

In some ways, this is easier in a world of scarcity than it is in a world of abundance. We have a copy of Mrs. Beeton's Book of Household Management (1861) on our family bookshelf. It includes remedies for everything from drunkenness to cholera, with treatments ranging from coffee to something called a turpentine stupe.

If I could have afforded a copy of the excellent Mrs. Beeton's book in 1861, I would have had no way of knowing where Mrs. Beeton got her information. I wouldn't have known why she chose to recommend the turpentine stupe. But if I were sick and unable to get to a doctor, I would have had a simple choice: to do or not do what she told me to do.

Today, when I need to address an illness, instead of standing over a turpentine stupe and wondering if it is a good idea, I'm staring at an endless pile of suggestions. We need to embrace the uncertainty of all that abundance and learn to cope as best we can.

The following practices for learning in abundance are by no means meant to be exhaustive. How could they be in a world of an abundance of connection? But I plan to add more practices to the book's companion website, http://learninginabundance.com/, in the future.

Practice 1. Build New Fact Habits

Each time you point to something that is true or a fact or "the way things are," take some time to check it. I suggested earlier that Wikipedia is a nice generic place to start, not because it tells the "truth" but because it's connected. Each article has links to the issues/topics/conversations that you are referring to.

Fortunately, the book on checking on facts has been written by Mike Caulfield at Washington State University. His book, *Web Literacy for Student Fact-Checkers and Other People Who Care about Facts*, published in 2017, explores the many ways in which people are trying to deceive you on the web and lays out four moves and a habit for making each of us better consumers of content. My favorite bit is about a habit that he suggests we all need.

The habit is simple. When you feel strong emotion—happiness, anger, pride, vindication—and that emotion pushes you to share a "fact" with others, STOP. Above all, it's these things that you must fact-check.

Why? Because you're already likely to check things you know are important to get right, and you're predisposed to analyze things that put you [in] an intellectual frame of mind. But things that make you angry or overjoyed, well . . . our record as humans are not good with these things. (7; ellipsis in original)

That habit, I think, is an adaptation that we need to make given all the information that we have around us. With the ease of publication on social media platforms, even casual thoughts that cross our minds get kept for posterity. I'm not so worried about what that's going to do for your future employability, though I have certainly looked at people's social media profiles as part of the hiring process. What I'm concerned with is how our casual acceptance of concepts or events that might be facts based on the way they make us feel strengthens those concepts or events.

If I happen to believe that ketchup is a tool of evil (which I do) and I see an article that supports my position, I'm going to send it along. Now if that article is simply saying that ketchup is the bane of culinary happiness and that it should be shunned as an insult to any cook, that's fine. I'm passing along something that is obviously an opinion. I have made it clear to whomever might be reading my stream that I'm a food snob and maybe a little obnoxious, but I've not supported my position with any weak or misleading facts.

If, however, the article suggests that ketchup causes some dread illness, that's a different story. Suddenly what I'm doing is adding my own trust to support a claim that is not true. Ketchup is disgusting, and I believe it will wreck your french fries, but I don't know that it causes any particular illness. And, more important, my thoughts on whether it makes people ill are irrelevant. But since it feels to me that it's probably true, as it matches my own disgust with the condiment, I'm happy to pass the disinformation along. If other people trust me, they are going to believe that I checked on the information to see whether it was true before I passed it along.

I feel strongly. It supports my opinion. *Share.*

We can all imagine issues far more important than ketchup that could be amplified by our passing information along. We, each of us, are part of the information-sharing and knowledge-making engine that is communication technologies in the twenty-first century. Because we're able to easily publish to a global audience, we are responsible in a way we have never been before for all our recorded utterances.

We need new habits for our everyday handling of truth. Being extra cautious when you are very excited about a fact, or a meme or whatever, is a great place to start.

Practice 2. Leave Bread Crumbs, Even in Casual Conversation

There isn't a debate on the internet nowadays that doesn't at some point include a person popping up and saying that they have done their "research." We talked a little bit about the difference between dishwasher research and actual research in a previous chapter. The recommendation here is simple. If you have "researched," or more likely read, something or have any reason to believe something, leave a trail to show how you came to your position. There is no need for any of us to claim knowledge of the politics in a foreign country or of some deep, obscure scientific theory or of a UFO landing. Simply post the source of your information. It can be as simple as a change of expression from "I did my research, and ketchup is a tool of the devil" to "Here is an article from *Mustard Daily* that says ketchup is a tool of the devil."

Reframing how you share information changes the nature of the conversation and the way your voice contributes to a conversation. It can change the nature of the way that we understand one another. In the first case, I'm starting an argument with you, but you have no idea of what my position is premised on. In the second case, you can see both my bias and the bias of the place I got my information.

This change can be difficult to make. Switching from "I believe" to "I believe what Heloise says" can impact our sense of identity and, frankly, just be hard to remember to do. Old habits are hard to break. Taking that extra time to check can also lead to us finding out that our long-held beliefs are things that are maybe not as certain as we thought they were.

Practice 3. Learn to Cheat Honestly. No Really, I Want You to Cheat

We're always borrowing our understandings from one another. We're always taking our guidance from others' work, either directly from them or from the things they've recorded in text or voice. We learn jokes from others. We take turns of phrase from TV commercials and expressions from our parents. We are mockingbirds.

When we move to a formal learning model, however, we have another word for it—we call it cheating. Look at the way we've been teaching through scarcity: we hide the answer from a student and ask them to figure it out or remember it. It's like we play hide-and-seek with the information. If we're going to use that model of teaching now, we have to create an artificial environment of scarcity. We have to turn off the internet search engines and AI systems. Block students from working with one another. Make them work by themselves. The technology is too good. Whether it's texts or math problems, anything that has a patterned response, anything where the teacher already knows the answer, is available to find or create online.

Schools are certainly moving to block students from using these things so they can prove that students are doing their own work. And yet, when we talk about being a productive citizen, we talk about how we need to collaborate and work together.

Forcing people to study by themselves is a troubling way to look at learning in a world of information abundance. There is little chance that any of us has had a purely original thought and certainly not a giant original thought. Our thoughts build on one another's. We collaborate. We hear things. We disagree with things. We steal other people's ideas. I mean you could say "borrow." You could say "learn from." You could say a lot of things, but the simple fact is that we learn things from one another.

The new advances in AI systems mean that any written text, any image, any video that you see could be created with the click of a button. This is going to happen. If you have the choice to use ChatGPT to summarize a one-hundred-page report or spend eight hours to do it yourself, most people are going to use ChatGPT most of the time. If we're honest about it, we can use our other skills to look for the biases that are built into these systems and allow others to do the same. Being transparent about our work, however we've done it, is more important than ever.

It's the same with your kid using these tools to learn. My kids do. But I try to get them to be honest about it. Try the math problem, struggle with it, use some AI system like MathGPT to help you when you're stuck. Talk to your teachers or your kids' teachers about it. Homework without these "helping" tools doesn't exist.

We need to learn to cheat honestly. Tell people where you learned what you learned. Build your learning collaboratively— that's the easiest way I've ever found to deal with abundance. Name the system that wrote your first draft. It can be a difficult model to adjust to, but it is a better reflection of the needs we have in the world we live in.

Practice 4. Be Gentle with Yourself and Your Beliefs as Time Passes

I think of learning as something we are built to do. It's our competitive advantage. The vast set of skills that you have now is not the same as the one you would have learned ten thousand years ago, and with good reason. We might see our inability to make a shoe or a fishing hook as a loss, but the challenges of an abundant world are, at least partially, different.

Maybe my favorite example is the ability to knap stone. Knapping is the process of chipping away at stone so that you can eventually get to the point where it can be used as a tool. You might use that tool for cleaning animal skins or chopping wood or settling an argument, but regardless, the right shape is critical. I am told that the skill required for knapping could take a lifetime to learn. Every piece of stone is different, requiring different handling to get to the desired shape. And being able to make good tools could mean the difference between life and death. Snack or no snack.

You, yourself, don't need to learn to knap stone. As soon as we started heating up metal into shapes, the stone knappers went out of style. Imagine being a stone knapper, Torg Knap from the family of knappers, leaders in your community because you've been the best knappers for generations, and, suddenly, your family skill is no longer top of the heap. Sure, people who couldn't afford metal still wanted your skills. It would have taken millennia, maybe, before those skills were no longer needed. But the tribe's relationship to your skill had changed. The power position changed. You weren't as valuable as you used to be.

We are at another changing of the guard. Metal. Houses. Writing. Print. Digital communications. At each of those points of transition, hundreds or sometimes thousands of years would pass as the culture slowly shifted to come to terms with the new reality. The fact that you make great tents? No longer relevant. You can remember *The Epic of Gilgamesh* in its entirety? Still cool, but not as necessary as before. You have a pile of monks in a building who will copy the writing of some long-dead person into another book? Meh. We're gonna roll off one hundred copies here on our Xerox machine. Or we're going to post this link, for free, without labor, to Facebook so our 1,600 "friends" can all access it.

I've argued here that the critical difference, the deep affordance, that our new technologies give us is an abundance of connection—connection to information, to people's ideas, to misinformation, to the world. That abundance exposes the uncertainty that has always hidden beneath the surface of our interactions. It used to be that you could know something and expect that that knowing would remain. And that's still true for many things. But increasingly, you could know something now, and five years later that knowledge will no longer be generally accepted among your peers.

The next new thing is always going to be just around the corner. That can create a lot of anxiety. We have fewer places in our lives where we can just accept that a certain thing is true, forever, leave thinking about it and move on. That feeling of falling behind, or not being able to keep up, is true for many of us. We can only accept that it's part of the new reality and find ways of learning the next new thing that work for us.

Practice 5. Learn to See Who Is Left Behind

The internet can also further separate the haves from the have-nots. If you can't afford to participate in the internet information revolution, you become further separated from the rest of the world. This book is a long-form discussion about the impact of the internet and abundance on how we think, but large portions of humankind are still not able, for reasons of structural inequality, to participate in that abundance, let alone in conversations about it.

Yet, in many parts of the world, public services are increasingly digital-first. Where I live, a person used to be able to walk into a government building or call a number and, by asking questions, find the service that they needed. The more we focus on digital services—and particularly the automated chatbot version of digital services—the less access we provide. People without devices are obviously impacted, but so are those who may not have the literacies to navigate complex digital bureaucracies and those whose questions are complex or don't fit the easy FAQ boxes that chatbots operate from. These issues disproportionately affect people who are poor, elderly, or marginalized—often the people most in need of public services.

The ways in which the internet and all its abundance work against us are not always transparent. In each case that we get something for free from a corporate platform, there is someone making money from it. Every time a public service gets provided in a new way, there are people who did it the old way who now face barriers or fall between the cracks. Neither that hidden profit nor those barriers are obvious in our abundant-information landscape. Indeed, the very abundance makes it harder to see.

It's important, however, at this juncture to do the work of learning to see the complex systems we rely on, and of thinking our way through what we pay for change. If we improve service at motor vehicle registrations, that's a net good, right? Nobody has to wait in line. Email is a faster version of mail. The internet is a vaster library. Zoom is—sometimes—a better telephone. These things are, in the broadest sense, true, but when a so-called improvement actually makes societal structures less accessible or less equitable, we need to address barriers and inequities rather than steam blithely ahead.

Digital technologies can be profoundly inequitable in their design and in their impact. Poor and racialized neighborhoods may face increased digital surveillance through police partnerships with Amazon Ring, while being overlooked for Wi-Fi network investment and upgrades. This means their citizens reap more risks than benefits from digital development. And when automated decision-making systems factor race, class, or age into a process, such as who is eligible for scholarships or food stamps, they categorize individuals based on the outcomes others of their demographic have experienced. This reinforces stereotypes and amplifies discrimination.

The tools themselves can also have racism baked into their core functions. A few months ago, I stood in a line at the airport while an automated facial recognition system checked white person after white person through the line. When a black woman stepped up to the camera, the system simply scanned up and down, failing to register her face. This has happened again and again with facial recognition tools, which—trained predominantly on white male faces—do not consistently recognize darker skin or accurately identify women.

And there are other examples. Many microphones don't pick up women's voices. Social media platforms enable hate speech. The microphones can be improved, if equity is valued, but the behavior of our fellow citizens on social media often does not reflect that principle.

We need to learn, in the midst of all this abundance, to see who our systems are leaving behind. And then we need to decide to care.

Practice 6. Model Your Values: Help Build a Prosocial Web

A few years ago, I was giving a presentation in a high school auditorium to parents about the internet. During the question period, one parent stood up, struggling to find the words to ask a question. She told a story about seeing her kids watch a mean-spirited YouTube video. She didn't know how to approach her children to address it. She talked about standing there, excluded, while her children laughed along with the video.

She asked me, "What am I supposed to do about the internet?"

Good question. What am I supposed to do about what the internet is doing to me? There was a terrible sense of helplessness in the way she spoke about the web. She saw it as something done *to* her. That mom was worried that she wasn't able or allowed to parent her children anymore. I tried, in a rambling ten-minute response, to give her permission to parent her kids, even if it's on the internet. I hope that what I said was that rules haven't changed, that we still can apply our own values to the internet. Things have just gotten harder.

Later that week, I ended up in a similar conversation with a colleague about kids' access to the internet. She mentioned that her child's access to the internet was limited to one hour a night and that the two of them were friends on Instagram. Without thinking, I asked, "You mean on the Instagram account you know about?"

I left that meeting thinking of all the things that a teenager could get into in an hour on the internet. In 2005, the concerns that I would have heard would have mostly been access to pornography and the potential of stalkers. As social sites became more and more prevalent, concerns in 2012 would evolve to include things like bullying in online spaces. A slightly savvier internet user would have suggested that things like 4chan were a danger.

The internet in 2024 has a whole other load of problems. There are deep algorithms that are tracking that child in the hour they are online, slowly crafting their desires toward some random purchase or pattern of behavior. The intensity of the attention economy has many of us—kids or not—convinced that we need to craft a personal image to an increasingly refined degree. The prevalence of digital devices has kids in constant emotional flux in their relationships with one another as they can change and shift on a minute-by-minute basis, often in the middle of the night. There are trolls, professional and otherwise, who are ready to attack for LOLs at any time. And,

maybe most dangerous, there are extremists (white national-
ists come to mind) who are actively recruiting young people
into some profoundly harmful ideologies. Plus, let's face it,
kids are constantly inundated by careless, petty microaggres-
sions by far too much of the adult population in their online
spaces.

But there is no way to keep children from the internet. There
is no conceivable process to keep any kid from the amazing potential of the internet. Guitar lessons on YouTube. Wikipedia
answers to fact-based questions. Recipes. Games with your
friends. Music . . . oh my god, the music. Almost anything you
could ever want to know or do can be found on the internet.

Kids are going to use the internet. Humans are going to use
the internet. We are going to learn all the lessons that the internet has to teach. We learn the pettiness and aggression. Just
think of the way people dismiss the feelings of famous people
by insulting them on the internet.

Here's the thing. *We can also affect what those lessons are.*

The internet is fundamentally participatory. The internet
grows, all internet platforms grow, through the addition of
content. Every time you post on Facebook or send a picture
into the ether, you've contributed to the conversation that is
shaping our future. Every comment. Every like. It shapes what
everyone else understands. Internet companies make money
(often from ads, sometimes from your data) when you participate in them.

The internet is people.

You can see where I'm going with this. The adults aren't coming. No one is going to "legislate" niceness on the internet.
They aren't going to make people say nice things, just as we don't
legislate that people have to be nice to one another in person.

We need to understand that we contribute to the larger voice every time we post . . . and every time we don't.

And I'm not talking about confronting trolls who are purposefully attempting to be aggressive or dismissive or vicious. You need to keep both your physical self and your emotional self safe. I'm talking about in the everyday way that we can be better with one another, with the people we know.

You need to help build a more prosocial web. Every time you are fair to someone you disagree with on the internet, you leave a good connection behind you. You create a participatory node that represents your values. Every time you fact-check something before you post it, and include the citation when you do, you're creating a reliable lesson that can be learned by someone else. Every time you participate in a conscious, deliberate way, you are putting another stone into the foundation that supports the values you believe in.

That is not to say that being prosocial is simply "making space for everyone." There are limits. Sometimes being prosocial means standing against something.

The last seven to eight years have shown us the tremendous impact that a cynical, extremist, and data-driven web can have on our culture. So many of these damaging, divisive culture wars are the creation of companies (and governments) with an agenda that has nothing to do with the well-being of our society.

Please participate. Do it well. Put your better values on the internet. Our society is literally being shaped by the internet right now and will be for the foreseeable future. We are all watching the web we're building. The web is us. Help build a good one.

The better we do, the more comfortable we'll become confronting uncertainty.

Practice 7. Take Time to Be Bored and to Care for Yourself and Others

The technologies around us change what is possible for us as societies. Some of those changes are amazing. Some of them are deeply troubling. Most of them could go either way. Is it bad that our kids can communicate with one another all the time? It can be. It depends on how we handle it.

One of the biggest things that the technology provides is access. Access to one another. Access to information we understand and information we can, probably, never understand. All that access can also take away that feeling of comfort that allowed us to feel like we understood the world we were living in.

But that certainty was always an illusion. The biggest difference is that now we see the uncertainty. The dominant cultural paradigms of my country—white, heterosexual, European descent, affluent, English-speaking (depending on where you live)—were never actually the only way that people lived. But they were the only ways that made it through the barrier of our media.

That barrier is gone.

We need to bring forward a new skill set if we're going to deal with both kinds of uncertainty: the kind that has been revealed by more voices being heard and the kind that has been caused by the changes that allowed those voices to be heard.

We need to have a conscious sense of our own values so we can use them to help inform our decisions. We have to understand who we trust and why we trust them. We need to be, in a small way, humble about the magnitude of all the things there are to know and understand our limits.

We need to use those skills to help us set limits too. We don't need to fill every moment with a blinking cursor or a notification. We can't work *all* the time or be connected *all* the time, so we need to talk to the people we love and figure out how to make time to be alone and quiet and bored while still being respectful of the people we are connected to.

Caring is always uncertain. It can often be hard. But I think it's worth it.

INDEX

boredom, 54, 110
brands and branding, 8–9, 137, 142, 143
bullying, online, 165

Caesar, Julius, 90
Canada, Truth and Reconciliation Commission, 139–40
Catholic Church, 91–92, 93
Caulfield, Mike, *Web Literacy for Student Fact-Checkers and Other People Who Care about Facts*, 155
cell phones: children's use of, 114–15; internet connectivity and, 31, 47, 65–66, 114–15; iPhone, 31; smartphones, 32, 114; use in remarketing, 79; values associated with use of, 33
certainty, 138, 168; as basis for learning, 137; desire for, 129, 147; ignorance-based, 59–60; loss of, 161–62, 168; regarding complex issues, 116. *See also* uncertainty
change, adaptation to, 19. *See also* technological change
Charlemagne, 93; "Charter of Modern Thought," 91–92
ChatGPT, 12, 72, 159
cheating, 158–60
Chi, Michelene, "Problem-Solving Ability," 133–34, 135
children, digital technology use of, 136, 164–66; cell phones, 114–15; internet-related hazards and, 165–66; as learning tools, 20; management of internet use, 164–65
climate change, 58, 62–63, 97, 107, 108, 134, 141
common sense, crisis of, 17–18, 74, 32, 74, 111
communities: connection to, 116–17; learning from, 14–15, 75, 116–17, 129, 134, 149; online, 116, 118–26; shared common sense of, 138

computers, 36–38, 47
consensus: in decision making, 148; scientific, 127–28
conspiracy theories, 59, 69, 128
corporations: brands and branding practices of, 8–9, 137, 142, 143; consumers' influence on, 141; and exploitation of information abundance, 6–7; internet data collection and use practices of, 76–83; profit motive, 162–63; role in culture wars, 167. *See also* marketing and advertising
COVID-19 pandemic, 109, 131–32, 153
creativity, 97, 132; boredom-related, 110; measurement of, 104; in problem solving, 97–98, 134; teaching of, 97, 103–4, 134
cultural factors: in interpersonal connections, 111; in parenting, 148; in pressure to express opinions, 6
cultural narratives: about internet use, 13; about material abundance and scarcity, 42
cultural paradigms, 168
culture(s): impact of fake news on, 72; impact of information abundance on, 13; impact of internet on, 10; Indigenous, 139–40; and privileged groups, 20, 90, 117–18, 131, 135, 138; relation to education systems, 87–88, 93; social norms of, 113
culture wars, 167
cuneiform, 90–91
curriculum: community as, 15, 75, 117, 129, 134, 149; exclusiveness of, 117; traditional educational, 9, 88–89

data collection on the internet, 75–83; and data sharing, 76, 78; and data tracking, 10, 11–12, 77; "free" services–based, 79–80, 82;

misuse of, 76, 82–83; for profit
motive, 10, 75–83; for research,
75–76, 79, 80
De Beers company, 7–8, 16–17
Decad, 91
decision making: in democracies,
141; digital information-based,
61–63, 66, 67; about educational
technology, 125–26; evidence-
based, 106; fake news and, 72;
information abundance and,
4–5, 50–51, 58, 82–83, 145–49;
information scarcity and, 67;
misinformation-influenced,
83, 141; and need for context,
126–27; process, 61–63; about
technological change, 29–30, 32;
uncertainty in, 137, 138; values-
based, 145–47, 168. *See also*
problem solving
Dellinger, Justin, 125–26
democracy/democracies, 141, 145
digital leadership, 111–12
digital technology, 161; collaborative learning and, 158–60; inequitable design of, 163–64. *See also*
cell phones; information abundance; internet
Dill, Senator, 26–27, 28
discrimination, 140; age-based,
136, 163; gender-based, 140,
163–64; racial, 136, 140, 163–64
Doxtdator, Benjamin, 123–24

education: definition of, 90; differentiated from learning, 87–89;
mandatory, 11
educational systems: bureaucrati-
zation, 97; change models, 88;
extrinsic motivators, 102–3;
historical overview, 90–93;
honesty in use of digital learning
tools, 158–60; intrinsic motivators, 103; memorization goal,
90–91, 103; monastery schools,
91–92; obstacles to change in,

88–89; power dynamics, 117;
practice-based learning approach,
85–86, 88, 90–91; religion and,
91–92, 93, 94–95; standardization goal, 90–91, 92, 93, 151;
teachers' roles, 86, 88, 92, 98, 99,
102; values, 90–93. *See also* grades
and grading; learning; teaching;
tests and testing; universities
educational technology, 125–26
email, 12, 31, 76, 112, 153, 163
encyclopedias, 37, 39; *Encyclopedia
Britannica*, 46, 64. *See also*
Wikipedia
energy use, climate change and,
42–43
English language, teaching of, 1–3, 98
evidence-based learning, 97, 104–8
Ewen, Stuart, *PR! A Social History of
Spin*, 7–8
expertise, 85
Eye, Glenn, "As Far as Eye Can See:
Knowledge Abundance in an
Environment of Scarcity," 43,
47, 48

Facebook, 49, 83, 139; advertising
on, 15–16, 39, 79, 82, 83; role in
information abundance, 6, 12,
24, 30, 161, 166; social implications of, 111–12, 128
face-to-face interactions, comparison with digital technology-
based interactions, 109–11, 113,
119, 121–22. *See also* friends and
friendship
facial recognition systems, 163–64
fact-checking, 20, 121, 127, 128,
147, 155–57, 167; emotions and,
155–56; research documentation
as, 123–24, 143–44, 157–58, 160,
167
facts, 5, 50, 57, 60–61, 94, 121,
166; differentiated from uncertainty, 139; as evidence, 105; false,
malicious, or misleading, 63, 72,

facts (*cont.*)
 108, 128, 156; use in decision
 making, 57, 62–63, 72
fake news, 68–72
formative assessment, 100–101
4chan, 165
Fox News, 119
Friedman, Thomas, 124
friends and friendship, 12, 107,
 111–12; digital compared with
 face-to-face connections, 111–13,
 119; on Facebook, 79, 111–12;
 as information sources, 15, 65,
 90; internet-based access and,
 112–15, 118–19; negative posts
 about, 73; responsibilities
 toward, 73, 111–12

gender: discrimination based on,
 140, 163–64; pronouns related
 to, 146–47
Gladwell, Malcolm, 85
Glaser, Robert, "Problem-Solving
 Ability," 133–34, 135
Google, 12, 15, 20, 34, 37, 48, 51,
 52–53, 58, 60, 120, 123; advertising based on, 79, 82; Docs, 12;
 Maps, 10; tracking of searches
 on, 77, 79
GPT-4 machine learning tool, 144
grades and grading, 77, 86, 97, 99,
 102, 103, 104
Gutenberg, Johannes, 46

hackers, 76
Harvard Business Review, 85
hate speech, 164, 165–66
"Hello" (Adele), 30
housing crisis, 135–36
humanism, 96, 97
humanities, 96
humility, 139, 145

identity: beliefs and, 158; digital,
 75, 81
Industrial Revolution, 24

inequalities: in digital technology
 applications, 163–64; in information access, 140, 162–63; racial,
 140, 163–65
information: creation, 48; differentiated from knowledge, 49–53;
 multiple sources of, 67
information abundance, 41–55;
 comparison with material abundance, 41–44; impact on learning
 and knowledge, 44–55, 72–73,
 158–60; implication for decision
 making, 61–63, 82–83, 140–41;
 and inequality of access, 140,
 162–64; as obstacle to learning,
 57–83; printed materials–based,
 44–46; responsibility for response
 to, 20, 111–12, 128–29, 134, 140,
 157; as transformational change,
 45–48, 160–62. *See also* internet;
 technological change
information access, 9–10, 141, 168;
 inequities in, 140, 162–64
information scarcity, 44, 48, 52–53,
 73; artificial, as learning environment, 158–60; decision making
 and, 59, 67; learning and, 20, 21,
 54–55, 98, 139, 158–60; as teaching model, 158–60
information sharing: fact-checking
 prior to, 155–57; formative assessment model, 101; internet connectivity and, 114; in learning, 159; of
 misinformation, 68–73
Instagram, 6, 14, 73, 165
internet: adaptation to, 47; connectivity, 34–35, 47, 65–66, 161;
 "free" services on, 79–80; impact
 on decision making, 4–5; impact
 on learning, 1–6, 52; impact on
 teaching, 1–4; negative comments on, 73–75; participatory
 nature of, 166–67; prosocial,
 164–67; reliability of information
 on, 63–64, 141–42; as transformational change, 4, 10–11, 38, 47

journalism and journalists, 19, 66, 68

knowledge: differentiated from information, 49–53; humanists' evaluation of, 96; uncertainty-based, 59, 60
knowledge machine, 37–40, 57, 64, 72

Latin language, 91–92
Lawrence, Jerome, *Inherit the Wind*, 23, 25, 29
learner engagement model, 103
learning: artificial information abundance and, 158–60; canonical basis of, 94–96, 97, 98–99; collaborative learning approach to, 158–60; community-based, 15, 75, 116–17, 129, 134, 149, 158; computer-based, 36–39; definitions and meanings of, 21, 86–87, 89, 105–6, 151–52; differentiated from education, 87–89; evidence-based, 97, 104–8; extrinsic motivation for, 102–3; fact-checking approach to, 155–57; formative assessment model of, 100–101; generational junctions in, 18–19; humanist tradition in, 96, 97; impact of internet on, 1–6, 52; informal, 18, 55, 158; as innate ability, 160; intrinsic motivation for, 103–4; listening as, 45; measurement of, 97, 98–106; memorization-based, 11, 14, 45, 94, 97–99, 105–6, 137, 148; misuse of, 89–90; personalized, 12, 77; practice-based, 85–86, 88, 90–91; research documentation for, 157–58; Scholastic tradition in, 94–96, 97, 104, 116; and shorthand approach for complex ideas, 152–53; strategic compliance in, 103; summative assessment

model of, 10, 100, 101–2; transitional technology changes and, 160–62
Lightfoot, Gordon, "The Wreck of the Edmund Fitzgerald," 51
listening as learning process, 45
literacies, twenty-first century: humility, 139, 145; informed trust, 141–45; values in decision making, 145–47
literacy as reading for knowledge, 45–46

Macedonia, 68, 69–70
machine learning, 144. *See also* artificial intelligence
marketing and advertising, 71, 138–39; data collection and use practices of, 16–17, 58–59, 76–83, 166; development of, 7–8; medical, 15–16; remarketing, 79; targeted, 15–16, 19, 58–59, 79, 81–83; of technological innovations, 11–12
Marvel movies, 95
MathGPT, 159
medicine and medical practice: impact of information abundance on, 13–16; uncertainty of, 138–39
memorization-based learning, 11, 14, 45, 94, 97–99, 105–6, 137, 148
Mesopotamia, scribal schools (eduba) of, 90–91, 93, 99, 151
misinformation and disinformation, 20; artificial intelligence-generated, 71–72; book-based, 63; and fake news, 68–70; implication for decision making, 83, 141; in information processing, 50–51; opinions as, 156–57; paper publications–based, 63, 70–71; politically oriented, 83, 145; profit-oriented, 83; targeted, 10

newspapers: comment sections of, 73; informed trust in, 142–43; political perspectives and, 19, 142; as reliable information source, 17, 19, 65

Nippur, 91

occupations, future changes to, 122–24

online community learning, 118–19

opinions: based on lack of knowledge, 59–60, 153; declining to express, 139–40, 153; as misinformation, 156–57; multitude of, 4; pressure to express, 6, 59–60, 153; reliable, 145; about research findings, 67–68; responsibility for, 157; sharing of, 156–57; of students, 132–33

paper, use in educational environments, 41–42. *See also* books and paper-based publications

Papert, Seymour, 35–36; knowledge machine concept of, 36–40, 57, 64, 72; *Mindstorms: Children, Computers, and Powerful Ideas*, 36

Pestalozzi, Johann Heinrich, 45, 93; *How Gertrude Teaches Her Children*, 93

political correctness, 118

political pamphlets, 70

political parties' exploitation of information abundance, 6–7

politics: factionalization of, 70, 108, 112; newspapers' political orientations, 142; as public interactions, 112; use of fake news and misinformation in, 13, 68–70, 81, 83; use of internet in, 71

Pompeii, 70

pornography, 165

power and power structures, 140, 161; internet-based, 71; political

correctness and, 118; privilege and, 27, 90, 118; and response to change, 24, 29

printing press, 4, 44–46, 47, 55, 70, 161

privacy, 18, 23, 25, 29–30, 107, 110

privilege, 131; expertise and, 85; gender- and race-based, 117–18; of power, 27, 90, 118; uncertainty and, 131, 135, 138

problem solving, 30, 31, 32, 33, 36–39; of classroom problems, 133–34, 135; creativity in, 97–98, 134; information scarcity and, 20; learning and, 99; of real-life problems, 133, 134–37. *See also* "right" answer approach to learning and problem solving; uncertainty-associated (real-life) problems

pronouns, personal choice in, 146–47

public services, internet-based barriers to, 163

questions: complex, inability to get answers to, 4–5, 60–63, 107–8, 127, 147–48, 154; with factual answers, 5, 10, 12, 13, 37–38, 60–61, 94, 147, 166; simple *versus* complex, 60–61. *See also* "right" answer approach to learning and problem solving; uncertainty-associated (real-life) problems

race and racism, 37, 117, 136, 139–40, 163–64

racial profiling, 136

radio, 9, 18, 19

reading, 66, 93; differentiated from research, 139; misuse of, 89–90; of research literature, 125, 126; role of, in learning, 45, 46, 100, 145

reality: information abundance–
based changes to, 12–13, 17–20,
161–62; marketing-based, 7–8
recipes, 51–53, 57, 139, 166
Reddit, 120
redlining, 136
religion's influence on educational
systems, 91–92, 93, 94–95
religious texts, 94–95
research: checks and balances in,
127–28; data collection for, 79,
80; differentiated from reading,
139; documentation of sources,
123–24, 143–44, 157–58, 160,
167; evaluation of, 11, 66;
evidence-based, 106; failure to
read, 125, 126; formal/profes-
sional, 58, 59; internet-based
(dishwasher-type), 58–59, 71,
140–41, 157; medical, 16, 17; new
approaches to, 145; quantitative,
107; traditional skills of, 46, 145;
uncertainty in, 139; understanding of, 67–68
"right" answer approach to learning
and problem solving, 9, 20–21,
37, 99, 102, 103, 116, 133–34;
best answer approach *versus*,
153–54; collaborative learning
approach and, 158–60; communities of belief and, 122, 124–25;
complex questions and, 37–40,
60–63, 107–8, 127, 154
Rittel, Horst, "Dilemmas in a
General Theory of Planning,"
133, 134–35
Rome, ancient, 70, 90, 96

Sacco, Justine, 74–75
Schlechty, Phil, 103
Scholasticism, 94–96, 104, 116
science, 138; distrust of, 72; response to COVID-19 pandemic,
131–32; uncertainty of, 138–39
search engines, 39, 57, 77, 158

Silverman, Craig, 68
Simon and Garfunkel, "America," 54
soccer, 60–63, 67, 72, 116, 127, 135
social interactions: formative
learning through, 100, 101–2;
learning through, 75; rules of, 75.
See also friends and friendship;
societal implications of information abundance
social media, 29, 48, 156; negativity
of posts on, 73–75, 164
social media services, 76
social messaging, 57–58
social norms, 113; of digital-based
social interactions, 111, 115,
120–21; education and, 87–88,
90–93; relation to material
abundance and scarcity, 42–43
societal implications of information
abundance, 12–13, 47, 109–29;
digital *versus* face-to-face interactions and, 109–11, 112, 113, 119,
121–22; loss of interpersonal
connections, 52–54; negativity
of internet posts, 73–75; online
communities and, 118–26; responsibilities and, 20, 111–12, 128–29,
134, 140, 157; social inequities,
162–64; unlimited interpersonal
connectivity, 113–16
song lyrics, 30, 46, 51, 57, 116
standardization in education and
learning, 90–91, 92, 93, 151
Star Wars movies, 95
St. Augustine, 92
stone knapping, 160–61
surveillance systems, 163–64
Syrian refugee crisis, 60

teachers: as information authorities, 11, 86; roles in educational
systems, 86, 88, 92, 98, 99, 102
teaching: information scarcity
model, 158–60; online *versus*
textbook-based, 1–4

technological change, 11–12, 23–40; and behavioral effects, 12, 33; decision making about, 29–30; economic beneficiaries of, 11–12, 23–24; entrepreneurs of, 11–12; frustration associated with, 24, 25–28, 30; incremental, 30–32; as job loss cause, 28, 29; power dynamics of, 24, 27, 28, 29, 31; social inequities associated with, 162–64; thought leaders on, 23–24; transformational, 4, 47, 160–62
technological determinism, 29
telemarketers, 32
telephone, 16, 18, 52; and technological innovations, 25–28, 30, 31, 32, 47, 120–21
Tesla, 24
tests and testing, 14, 79, 86, 92, 94, 97, 102, 103, 104, 105–6, 115
text, AI system–generated, 144, 159
textbooks, 1–2, 3, 38, 46, 93, 117; comparison with online teaching, 3; development of, 46; exclusiveness of, 117
texting, 25, 31, 109, 110, 112, 159; etiquette of, 17, 33, 111, 114, 115, 120; relationships built on, 120
thinking: about technological change, 4, 163; in decision making, 72; independent, 133; linear, 103; in problem solving, 153–54; procedural, 36–37
thought control, 92, 93
thought leaders, 23–24, 124
Trump, Donald, 69, 70
trust: in authorities as information and knowledge sources, 4–5, 11, 13, 60, 63, 108, 124, 127, 138, 141, 158, 168; informed, 141–45, 148–49; in news media, 19
truth, 20; canonical, 94–96; evaluation of, 66; factionalized, 108; marketing-based, 7–9;

objective, 5; online communities' versions of, 120–21, 124–25; universal, 139
Truth and Reconciliation Commission of Canada, 139–40
Turkle, Sherry, *Alone Together*, 109, 110, 116
Twitter, 50, 73, 128

uncertainty, 107, 131–49; certainty *versus*, 116; change-related, 29; COVID-19 pandemic–related, 131–32; differentiated from fact, 139; exploitation of, 6–7; information abundance–related, 6, 11, 48, 112; knowledge-based, 59, 60; in learning, 21, 98; of medical practice, 16; of online conversations, 140; pre-internet, 137–38; privilege and, 131, 135, 138; in science and medicine, 138–39; students' preparation to deal with, 132–33; in teaching, 1–3, 4; values and, 146–47, 148–49, 168
uncertainty-associated (real-life) problems, 21, 37–38, 108, 133, 134–37, 149; compared with classroom-type problems, 133–34; example, 60–63; fact-checking approach to, 155–57; information scarcity and, 154; "right" answer *versus* best answer approach to, 153–54
United States Senate, rotary telephone debate in, 25–28, 30, 31
universities: founding, 92; humanist tradition of, 96; Scholastic tradition of, 94–96; thought control in, 92, 93
University of Paris, 44, 45, 92
University of Texas at Arlington, LINK Research Lab, 125
University of Toulouse, 44, 45